T0306176

THE BASICS OF
PROCESS
IMPROVEMENT

Praise for *The Basics of Process Improvement*

The difference between good and great is not quality or productivity, it is the way you run your processes. If you follow these suggestions about basic process improvement you will maximize the value of your output to all stakeholders. This book embodies the fundamentals and reminds us all of the key techniques for success.

—*H. James Harrington, prolific author of more than 35 process improvement books, CEO, Harrington Institute*

Every journey begins with a first step, and the path to better work process is no different. *The Basics of Process Improvement* gives the beginning practitioner all the tools needed to start their path towards a better way. Every step in your journey will be enhanced by the practical insights and proven approaches offered inside. Now get on your way!

—*Rich Sheridan, author of* Joy, Inc.: How We Built a Workplace People Love; *CEO, chief storyteller, Menlo Innovations*

Rather than evangelizing yet another methodology, *The Basics of Process Improvement* offers actionable ideas and step-stair approach that can be immediately applied. Concepts such as the "process-oriented architecture" introduced and explained by the authors' meaningful framework for scaling-up to enterprise-wide process improvement. It is a highly useful learning guide and road map appropriate for professional practitioners and internal consultants.

—*Nathaniel Palmer, editor of* BPM.com *and author of* Passports to Success in BPM

Cardella and Boutros have captured the fundamentals of process improvement in an easy-to-read and relatable book. With deep roots in formal methodology, they refresh us with the simplicity of applied improvement principles for both novice and expert while keeping true to success with focus on pragmatic delivery and real-life application. An excellent reference book for all.

—*Tim Purdie, coauthor of* The Process Improvement Handbook

Process improvement remains at the heart of business success in the best of economic times and has even greater importance in the face of economic uncertainty and the digital age. If you want to know the best way to do it, don't forget the basics. The examples in this book will certainly start your creative juices flowing and help your organization transform and mature.

—*Peter Fingar, author of* The Insiders' Guide to BPM: 7 Steps to Process Mastery *and* Business Process Management (BPM): The Next Wave

Tristan and Jen's new book, *The Basics of Process Improvement,* is a refreshing and long-overdue publication that is certainly going to be welcomed by many business readers. Business analysts and process analysts at all levels of an organization will find that this book provides a single and concise repository for some of the world's most well-known and effective process improvement tools. With so many methodologies to choose from, it can be hard for a process improvement practitioner to locate and apply the right methodology for their projects. My advice is to follow Tristan and Jen's guidance and stick to the fundamentals. They have taken great care to explain each methodology, why they're effective and how to apply them in a project context. I have no doubt that readers will find *The Basics of Process Improvement* and that it will remain a relevant and highly effective source of knowledge for many years to come.

—*Theodore Panagacos, author of* The Ultimate Guide to Business Process Management

In a world of competing confusions it is refreshing to get back to the foundations of process. And this book does a fantastic job of reminding us of the core principles that underpin all process thinking. In an easy-to-understand jargon-free walk-through, readers from all levels will enjoy the no-nonsense insights and techniques that produce practical immediate results. In this customer-centric world, process has never been more important as a critical part of business success, so let Boutros and Cardella renew your love of process to help deliver personal, business, and customer success.

—*Steve Towers, author of* The Process Tactics Playbook *and* A Senior Executive's Guide to Business Process Reengineering; *CEO, BP Group*

Beginning our education in process improvement and operational excellence can feel like a daunting task. There are so many books one could read, outlining so many concepts and principles that we need to understand. Boutros and Cardella have done an amazing job compiling the essentials and fundamentals of process improvement, operational excellence, and creating a continuous improvement culture. This book provides a great overview for readers, as it outlines concepts and explains the toolkit required to begin with the fundamentals of process discipline.

—*Robert Martichenko, author of* Everything I Know about Lean I Learned in First Grade *and* Lean Six Sigma Logistics: Strategic Development to Operational Success

Process improvement may be one of the most important concepts for all organizations. Tristan and Jennifer have put together a book which will help any individual or organization understand and implement this important approach. It brings together some of the key concepts and tools for process improvement while showing how these can be used in the real world. The range of tools will be invaluable for anyone who is tasked with ensuring process improvement exists in the organization and for those for whom process improvement is a part of their job. And the breadth and depth of the discussion will allow those who are new to process improvement an introduction to the tools, while ensuring those who are experienced a chance to learn more.

—*Mike Jacka, author of* Business Process Mapping: Improving Customer Satisfaction

Some people use the phrase "Keep it simple stupid" (KISS), but there's nothing stupid about keeping things simple! Simplicity looks easy. It's not. It's much easier to complicate than simplify. Simplicity helps strip away the irrelevance in your work; it will have no waste, no weakness and no flaws—this is the beauty of simplicity. It could enable you to permanently and radically change the world, but starting with your own organization and its processes would be a good first step! That's where this book comes into play, providing a message for managers to take responsibility for making their processes much simpler, both for their employees and the customers.

—*John Morgan, author of* The Lean Six Sigma Improvement Journey, Go Lean, Lean Six Sigma for Dummies, *and* Lean Six Sigma Business Transformation for Dummies

It's easy to fall into the trap of overcomplicating process management, but both authors stay true to the fundamentals, and there are two themes explored that stand out here: the application of commonsense approaches to managing complex processes and BPM project success, and the impact on workforce culture, a topic a lot of process improvement books miss out. These alone make this book worthy.

—*Theo Priestley, technology evangelist, speaker,* Forbes *contributor, former chief technology evangelist at Software AG*

The authors take a refreshing and holistic approach to the subject of process improvement. For IT leaders who are jaded from the barrage of disconnected and oftentimes very sophisticated "shiny objects" that don't deliver on their promises, the book is a welcome relief in the way it covers simple yet effective tools. The authors take pains to relate the use of these tools to the wider requirements of success in implementing process improvement initiatives, such as process thinking as a cultural change, project methodology, new skills and competencies, and alignment with the business. I am confident this book will serve as a constant desk reference for the serious professional.

—*Kiran Garimella, author of* The Power of Process: Unleashing the Source of Competitive Advantage *and* BPM Basics

Warning: Do not pick up this book if you don't want to improve! Boutros and Cardella bring tried and true practices, as well as new, novel approaches to those wishing to improve processes within their organizations. Combined with common sense and a pragmatic approach, learn how you can incrementally improve processes every day!

—*Stacia Viscardi, author of* The Professional Scrum Master's Handbook

Boutros and Cardella bring process improvement back! Today's adaptive digital enterprise must aim to harmonize the interactions between people, process, and corresponding technologies. Revitalizing a culture of continuous process improvement, they brilliantly bring process back into focus with practical methods to consistently plan, grow, and innovate in a highly fluid environment.

—*Shahan Khoshafian, technology thought leader and account executive, Pegasystems*

Business process improvement and management (BPM) activities have significantly evolved over the last 10–15 years. While there have been many books written on the topic, there are few that are detailed enough to inform you how to execute BPM projects, and yet pragmatic enough to take account of an organization's differences. This book does not fall into this trap. This book provides practical tools and techniques to enable successful projects to be competed. Yet, it blends the practicalities of the "real" world of business and organizational and project differences. Couple this book with my book on the 7FE BPM Framework and you will have all the information you will need to be successful in a process-led organizational business transformation program.

—*John Jeston, author of* Business Process Management *and* Management by Process

The Basics of Process Improvement provides the much needed foundation for all levels in an organization to learn and apply critical skills to meet the increasing speed of change in today's demanding business environments.

—Brent Drever, CEO, Acuity Institute

Awareness of the process improvement concepts contained in this book is paramount to effective organizational leadership and management.

—Paul Keller, author of The Six Sigma Handbook: A Complete Guide for Green Belts, Black Belts, *and* Managers at All Levels

In this seminal book, Tristan Boutros and Jennifer Cardella expand upon the foundations of process improvement, balancing well-tested transformation disciplines with Lean management trends.

—Setrag Khoshafian, author of Service Oriented Enterprises; *chief evangelist and vice president of BPM Technology, Pegasystems*

THE BASICS OF
PROCESS
IMPROVEMENT

Tristan Boutros
Jennifer Cardella

Illustrations by Dustin Duffy

CRC Press
Taylor & Francis Group
Boca Raton   London   New York

CRC Press is an imprint of the
Taylor & Francis Group, an **informa** business

A PRODUCTIVITY PRESS BOOK

Illustrations by Dustin Duffy

CRC Press
Taylor & Francis Group
6000 Broken Sound Parkway NW, Suite 300
Boca Raton, FL 33487-2742

© 2016 by Taylor & Francis Group, LLC
CRC Press is an imprint of Taylor & Francis Group, an Informa business

No claim to original U.S. Government works

Printed on acid-free paper
Version Date: 20160330

International Standard Book Number-13: 978-1-4987-1988-9 (Paperback)

Library of Congress Cataloging-in-Publication Data

Names: Boutros, Tristan, author. | Cardella, Jennifer, author.
Title: The basics of process improvement / by Tristan Boutros and Jennifer Cardella.
Description: Boca Raton, FL : CRC Press, 2016. | Includes bibliographical references and index.
Identifiers: LCCN 2015045135 | ISBN 9781498719889
Subjects: LCSH: Reengineering (Management) | Workflow--Management. | Process control. | Quality control.
Classification: LCC HD58.87 .B68 2016 | DDC 658.4/063--dc23
LC record available at http://lccn.loc.gov/2015045135

Visit the Taylor & Francis Web site at
http://www.taylorandfrancis.com

and the CRC Press Web site at
http://www.crcpress.com

This book is dedicated to our children, Preston and Alexandra. Your growth provides a constant source of joy and pride. We have made the sacrifices that we have so that your futures are brighter, and you are the reason we wake up everyday and want to do more, be more, and make a difference in this world. This book and all future books are for you both.

Contents

Forewords

Technology advances are having a tremendous impact on businesses. Today, the only option for being current and viable is to become a digital business. From a technological perspective, these advances mean disruptive megatrends in connectivity, social networking, Internet of Things, Big Data analytics, cloud computing, and mobility. But there is more. Pursuing these "shining" balls and chasing the most recent technology or buzzwords without the foundations for transformation is similar to building one's house on sand. To have a solid foundation that can withstand disruptive trends, businesses need to build upon the core fundamentals (solid "rocks") of efficiency and effectiveness.

In this seminal book, Tristan Boutros and Jennifer Cardella expand upon the foundations of process improvement, balancing well-tested transformation disciplines with Lean management trends. This balance is key for the success of adaptive digital enterprises. Driving transformation and innovation, while embracing well-proven disciplines of process improvement, is not an easy task.

The difficulty emanates from several core challenges:

- Faster and more agile businesses: Simplifying technology portfolios with fewer data centers, platforms, and applications improves information technology (IT) efficiency and aligns business and IT. Modernizing applications with digitalization addresses the very core of the complexity challenge by enabling IT and business to rapidly respond to the need for change.
- Optimization of value streams: Business transformation will increase transparency, visibility, and control of the value stream. Adaptive enterprises are realizing that the end-to-end chain of value work assigned to different units is as strong as the weakest link. The entire stream needs to be digitized and optimized—not just individual links within business units.
- Demanding customers: The new generation of customers is increasingly demanding. They want to be treated differently— "special." Furthermore, social networking channels have given

them a powerful voice, allowing them to instantly provide feed-back (good and bad) and share ideas about products, services, and companies.

- The rise of things: From wearables to smart homes and cities, to connected cars, to digital devices in transportation, utilities, and manufacturing, the connectivity of humans that was launched through the Internet revolution is about to explode with a massive network of connected sensors and actuators. The Internet of Things is uniquely addressable physical devices over the Internet. Things, of course, are manufactured and increase the level of connectivity between the manufacturer and consumer. The Internet of Things is disrupting process improvement in all industries: manufacturing, energy, transportation, insurance, and healthcare—to name a few—with smart and connected devices in processes.

So it is with this background that the authors embark on the difficult task of elucidating the process improvement foundations while encouraging innovation for adaptive digital enterprises. This book will empower you with pragmatic process improvement tools. It is comprehensive and prescriptive. For process improvement tools, it covers a diverse yet focused list of techniques, such as the 5 Whys, Pareto charts, and strengths, weaknesses, opportunities, and threats (SWOT) analysis.

Process improvement needs to be holistic. Modern enterprises are incorporating both structured process flowcharts and dynamic cases—especially with social and ad hoc interactions. The book also delves into process architectures and, most importantly, process-oriented architecture—where processes, together with humans, data, roles, enterprise applications, and business partners, become participants in end-to-end processes. Through a clear articulation of proven process improvement approaches, this book is a reference toolkit for success. It is an important and seminal work. Taken to heart, it could help adaptive digital enterprises embark on digital innovation initiatives while avoiding waste, improving customer experiences, and keeping their processes in control.

Setrag Khoshafian
Author of Service Oriented Enterprises; *chief evangelist
and vice president of BPM technology, Pegasystems*

Process! Process! Process! Like location to real estate, process is the key to an organization's success. Organizations exist to serve a purpose, and process is the means by which the purpose is served. Process defines the execution of the organization's objectives, its interactions with customers, and its ability to convert input to output profitably, whether the output includes goods and services or services alone.

While empowerment of process-level employees with responsibility for ongoing process management and improvement sounds noble enough, it is fraught with potential disaster, simply because the process does not exist in a vacuum. Processes exist in systems, which consist of related processes, the various stakeholder groups that interact with and are impacted by these processes, and the equipment, materials, and environmental factors that influence the processes. System-level issues must remain a focal point of process management and change. Optimization of an individual process may well degrade the overall system performance, a notion popularized by W. Edwards Deming in the 1980s. Process-level employees, while responsible for implementing the process, often have little authority over the system-level factors noted above. Internally, these responsibilities will be delegated to other process-level personnel, support staff, and various levels of management. Externally, depending on the process, process-level employees may have little interaction with customers and suppliers. Even when they do, the communication may be of limited informational value, or otherwise provide a poor representation of the overall system requirements.

Deming frequently cited management's primary role in system-level improvement as the overall owner of the various processes and the systems in which they operate. Involvement of the key stakeholder groups is an unmistakable requirement. In recognition of these concerns, a notable contribution to the methods of process improvements is found in the practices known as Six Sigma (aka Lean Six Sigma), where improvement is achieved through cross-functional project teams, comprised of key stakeholder groups and sponsored by the functional system managers.

Yet, while a system-level approach with participation of key stakeholder groups and management is necessary, it is not sufficient for achieving sustainable process improvement. Improvement, by definition, implies a change from one state to another, more desirable state. Similarly, process management implies sustainability of the process at a desired state. In either case, it should be clear that the determination of the state of the process, historically or in its present condition, requires measurement, which in turn requires a means to evaluate the measurement. This is the realm of statistics. Shewhart developed the appropriate statistics for evaluating process measurements, statistical process control (SPC), in the 1920s. Deming introduced this tool to several generations and lamented the misuse of the more conventional enumerative statistics (i.e., confidence intervals and hypothesis tests) to process data. Through the use of SPC, process analysts can first assess the current state of the process, and then the state of the process after the improvement effort, to verify a sustained process improvement. The SPC control chart provides the operational definition of a process change: the special (aka assignable) cause indicated when the measured data plot outside the statistical control limits inherent to the process. Astute management should accept nothing short of this as evidence of process improvement, whether the improvement effort employs high-powered statistical tools or simple Lean concepts.

Critically, the control chart prevents the analyst from confusing the random variation inherent to the process with a real process change. As such, it is an essential tool in preventing unintentional degradation to the process (in the form of increased variation, which Deming termed process tampering). A variety of tools and techniques can then be applied to understand the fundamental causes of these two very distinct types of process variation, from simple problem solving to designed experiments and constraint theory, as detailed in this book.

It is human nature to improve one's state, and process improvement is a natural extension of this phenomenon. It is ongoing and perpetual, driven by customers' expanding expectations, shareholders' continued interests in profitability, and employees' motivations to meet these objectives with minimal anguish. Awareness of these process improvement concepts is paramount to effective organizational leadership and management.

Paul Keller

Author of The Six Sigma Handbook: A Complete Guide for Green Belts, Black Belts, *and* Managers at All Levels

Preface

Over the past several decades, our economy has witnessed significant and continual changes in technological speed and precision. There has been an information overload created by mobile computing, social networking, analytics, and cloud computing. The global population has expanded and customer expectations have changed, resulting in an often-continuous flow of unmet needs. Technology advances have produced new product and service offerings, and the structure of many industries has also transformed, with mergers and acquisitions turning competitors into unified companies. Yet, with all of those changes, the basic principles for managing innovation and organizational transformation have remained constant. Whether an enterprise is focused on efficiency gains, innovation, growth, cost containment, or customer satisfaction, embracing flexible processes and structures and adopting a culture of process improvement are essential ingredients for success.

Unfortunately, an increasing number of corporate projects and transformation initiatives forget the historical teachings and basic fundamentals of improvement, and fail to deliver their intended results or even compete successfully. Today's managers often try to apply sophisticated tools and technologies to deal with problems that can be solved with simple, commonsense approaches. All too often, business leaders are quick to jump on the latest technology trend or the latest-breakthrough business method to meet strategic objectives. Traditional process improvement is labeled as mundane or outdated, while technology advancements and breakthrough organizational strategies have become the new standard at business conferences and in executive circles. While technology theory and breakthrough industry trends hold key insights and are critical to organizational evolution, one important building block, that of practical implementation, is often lacking or missing altogether in corporate improvement efforts.

Another problem besetting many companies today is that process improvement is frequently considered to be synonymous with many quality programs or methodologies, such as Total Quality Management, Lean, Six Sigma, or Rummler-Brache. Many organizations believe that if they implement rigorous quality programs with teams of certified practitioners, the final result will undoubtedly be successful, and the elimination of problems will be inevitable. The tendency to place too much emphasis on a specific methodology, while disregarding fundamental values such as common sense, self-discipline, order, and economy, is another reason why many organizational improvement initiatives fail to succeed. Moreover, we continue to observe several other problems that lead to undesirable improvement outcomes. These include the following:

- Employees often lack the basic skills to see their work in a new way and improve how they work when needed.
- Organizations often rely on sophisticated technologies to solve everyday problems.
- Upper-level management often lacks an understanding of how process improvement can help support innovation and business transformation.
- Organizations often fail to link project objectives with corporate or business goals.
- Organizations often fail to engrain process-oriented thinking into their cultural values.
- Improvement efforts often optimize parts of the organization at the suboptimization of the greater enterprise.
- Business leaders often struggle to determine what project methodology to use or what problem-solving technique is relevant for the issues at hand.

Process improvement involves the entire organization, from the highest levels of management to those who are responsible for day-to-day operations. It focuses on solving problems with sound judgment and with technology as an accompanying tool. Organizations that focus solely on innovation, emerging technologies, or specific methodologies often forget to eliminate ancillary wastes or consider the human or organizational change element, costing them significant time and money. Companies need to understand how to organize themselves around innovation and how to get the best results from it. They must consider their strategic imperatives and how they can drive holistic transformation through people, process, and structure. The next step is to identify the technologies that are best suited to their unique circumstances. Top-performing companies show greater mastery in how they balance these change pillars in order to plan, innovate, measure results, interact with customers, and create value more efficiently.

To be competitive in today's global marketplace, organizations need to be driving innovation in their products and services through a combination of continuous and breakthrough improvement. This book is intended to show how process improvement is an essential building block that can keep enterprises grounded and assist with bringing about truly rewarding accomplishments. We believe that it is time to reintroduce the many simple, time-proven fundamentals that have been pushed into the background over the years. Supporting the basics of process improvement at the foundational core of innovation ensures organizations learn and improve together. Furthermore, leaders and practitioners alike must embrace process improvement, not just as a set of tools, but as an ongoing cultural value and pillar of their strategy. By doing so, organizations will be able to evolve more cost-effectively and enjoy a more consistent and predictable business model. This book serves as an outline for companies that wish to design and manage their processes and structures simply and effectively. By following basic practices and applying sound principles, any company can benefit from process improvement.

WHY WE WROTE THIS BOOK

Several excellent books oriented toward process and performance improvement, Lean, and Kaizen have been published in the past. These books are generally focused on helping the practitioner and are usually centered on a specific element of the discipline. We decided to write a book aimed at helping organizations be more successful at fixing basic operational issues and problems using a broad and wide-sweeping process-based toolkit. We want to help individuals who have worked in stale or siloed thinking enterprises to make the transition to a process or improvement-oriented culture, and teach those who are unfamiliar with process tools to look at their work with a new lens and adopt a continuous improvement and analytical thinking mindset. We have used the various methods, tools, and concepts found in this book to help solve practical, day-to-day problems at various organizations and put many of the tools into this book to help workers, managers, practitioners, executives, and anyone else with a stake in improving processes, operating cultures, or solving day-to-day working problems produce better products or services.

Process improvement practices are not limited to members of Lean or Six Sigma teams. They can be used to improve software development, facilitate analysis or brainstorming sessions, identify root causes of problems, test products or services, or improve workplace quality overall. This book serves to help process improvement practitioners working on projects using any type of improvement methodology. We enjoy process improvement because its values, principles, and core practices and techniques enable people to do their best work, and improvement and quality are central to process improvement.

AUDIENCE FOR THE BOOK

This book is for anyone who is, will be, or wants to be a part of a process improvement culture. Beginners and experienced readers alike should find the information they need to understand the basic activities required to manage process improvement initiatives. We believe that beginners to process improvement, those with no prior exposure to its various tools and techniques, or even seasoned professionals will find this book suitable to help successfully get process improvement activities up and running.

This is not a technical book with statistical formulas or complex analytical tools. Readers should open this text with open-mindedness, courage, honesty, and a willingness to take a hard look at themselves and their organization or industry, with the goal of identifying areas for improvement. If you don't wish to master process improvement, and just want to develop your critical thinking toolkit, or build a process-oriented perspective to ongoing work, this book is for you too. We attempt to use plain, straightforward language without caveats or digressions while including several practical tips. We candidly call out situations where items are and aren't appropriate and what alternatives may be considered.

Ultimately, this book is written for

- Managers responsible for ensuring quality, managing costs, ensuring safety, overseeing production of goods or services, or ensuring performance excellence
- Executives with strategic interest in process improvement and business transformation
- Quality, maintenance, process improvement, project management, engineering, architecture, technology, and human resources professionals

- Students engaged in management studies
- Anybody interested in process or operational excellence

There are many flavors of process improvement, but they all have much in common. Whether you are practicing Lean, Six Sigma, Rummler-Brache, or the various other widely used quality and improvement principles, you'll find information in this book to help with your efforts.

STRUCTURE OF THE BOOK

Before presenting the actual practices of process improvement, this book begins with introductory remarks and acknowledgments, and briefly describes the purpose and patterns found in the book.

- **Chapter 1** explores the basic values, principles, and practices of process improvement and describes the foundational concepts needed to improve productivity. It helps answer questions like
    - What is a process?
    - What is process improvement?
    - What are the benefits of process improvement?
    - What are the core values of process improvement?
    - What are the various phases of process improvement?
- **Chapter 2** presents the basics of process mapping and its benefits. It also outlines the various types of process maps and helps answer questions like
    - What is process mapping?
    - Why map a process?
    - What do process maps consist of?
    - What are the various types of process map?
    - What is the difference between process mapping and modeling?
- **Chapter 3** walks you through the five core phases of process improvement and describes a simple process improvement framework. Some of the key questions answered in Chapter 3 include
    - What is a process improvement framework?
    - What are the various stages of process improvement?

- **Chapter 4** introduces the concept of process architecture and outlines its relationship to various other architecture types. It helps answer questions like
  - What is process architecture?
  - What is process modeling?
  - What is process-oriented architecture?
  - How are process models managed?
- **Chapter 5** explores various tools and techniques for improving processes and how to overcome problem-solving barriers in the workplace. It helps answer questions like
  - What are some of the basic tools used for process improvement?
  - What are some of the more advanced practices used in process improvement?
- **Chapter 6** outlines the importance of organizational culture in improvement activities and how to develop and implement a process improvement strategy that works for your organization. It discusses the various changes required from leadership in a process-oriented environment and presents ideas to make your organization's culture as strong as it can be. It helps answer questions like
  - What is culture?
  - What is a process improvement culture?
  - How do I define the culture I want?
  - What are the various behaviors that impact culture?
  - How do I change the behaviors of others?
- **Chapter 7** summarizes the principles and concepts of the book and presents several key success factors process-oriented organizations can use for successful improvement. If you're having trouble deciding where to start with process improvement, or how to improve what you are doing now, these success factors will give you direction.
- We've also included a glossary we hope you will find useful, as well as references to books, articles, and websites in the bibliography.

HOW TO READ THIS BOOK

There are different ways to read this book, and you don't necessarily have to read the book in sequential order:

- If you are interested in a quick overview, just go through each chapter quickly, and read the various callouts outlined below. These form the quick-hit items that provide you with an overall impression of the chapter and book as a whole.
- Read the complete text if you want to gain the deepest insight and are particularly interested in the end-to-end idea of process improvement.
- Skip to any specific chapter to gain a deeper-level understanding of specific process improvement core knowledge areas.

This is a relatively short book and is intentionally lightweight. You don't have to read many hundreds of pages to gain basic understanding of the concepts contained in the text.

In this book, you will find two icons that distinguish between different kinds of information. Here are some examples of those icons and an explanation of their meaning:

Key Point: Denotes a key point for implementing process improvement successfully or highlights a technical detail regarding the discipline.

KEY POINT

Definition: Pinpoints the most important terms and concepts in the book. Pay attention to these for quick overviews on key terminology.

DEFINITION

In addition, a glossary of process improvement terms and concepts is provided at the back of the book. We have tried to call out all meaningful terms, concepts, and definitions throughout the text within that section.

HOW TO CONTACT US

Feedback from our readers is always welcome. Let us know what you think about the text, what you liked or may have disliked. Reader feedback is important for us to develop future editions or works that you will get the most out of. To send us general feedback, submit ideas for future editions, ask questions, or contact us about partnership, consulting, speaking, or training opportunities, please reach out and connect via our professional profiles:

- Tristan Boutros: https://www.linkedin.com/in/tristanboutros
- Jennifer Cardella: https://www.linkedin.com/in/jennifercardella

Additionally, please follow Tristan on Twitter @TristanBoutros and Jennifer @JenCardella for updates and related commentary.

Although we have taken every care to ensure the accuracy of our content, mistakes do happen. If you find a mistake in our book, we would be grateful if you would report this to us. By doing so, you can save other readers from frustration and help us improve subsequent versions of this book. If you find errata, please report them by emailing michael.sinocchi@taylorandfrancis.com. Once your errata are verified, your submission will be accepted and the errata will be uploaded on our website or added to a list of existing errata.

For more information about Productivity Press books, conferences, and resource centers, please visit their website at http://www.productivitypress.com.

Please address comments and questions concerning the physical book and its distribution or technical issues concerning the e-book format to

Taylor & Francis Group
7625 Empire Dr.
Florence, KY 41042
(800) 634-7064
orders@taylorandfrancis.com

We have a webpage for this book, where additional information can also be found: https://www.crcpress.com/product/isbn/9781498719889.

PIRACY

Piracy of copyrighted material is an ongoing problem across all media, and we take the protection of our copyright and licenses very seriously. If you come across any illegal copies of our works, in any form, please provide us with the location address or website name immediately so that we can pursue a remedy. Please contact us at michael.sinocchi@taylorand-francis.com with a link to the suspected material. We appreciate your help in protecting our works, fellow authors, and our ability to bring you valuable content.

Acknowledgments

The Basics of Process Improvement grew out of our passion for project management and continuous improvement. First and foremost, we want to acknowledge the people we work with that challenge our thinking, question our reasoning, and provide us with ideas and support. Special thanks go to Mike Jbara, Monica Jonas, Shawn McIntyre, Millie Cabrera, Mario Andreotti, Hunain Mahmood, Rizwan Hasan, Jeffrey Diego, Allison Reilly, Amy Lo, Nuria Fidalgo, Michael Boumansour, Christopher Barry, Roger Valade, Peter Romano, Jonathan Murray, Joe Braidish, Natacha Cordova, Andrew Polito, Robert Gass, Jacob Ahmu, Roger Gare, Tom Petriw, and Matt Lewry. Thank you for keeping us motivated.

Second, we want to thank fellow thought leaders in the process improvement arena. Without your knowledge sharing and support, this text would not be possible. In particular we thank

- Setrag Koshafian
- Paul Keller
- H. James Harrington
- Rich Sheridan
- Theo Priestley
- John Morgan
- Shahan Koshafian
- Peter Fingar
- Brent Drever
- Theodore Panagacos
- Steve Towers
- Robert Martichenko
- Mike Jacka
- Nathaniel Palmer
- Kiran Garimella
- Stacia Viscardi
- John Jeston

Thank you to all of the teachers along the way that took special notice of us and helped both of us get to this point in our careers. A special thank you to Dr. Ted Vokes and Mr. Bob Loebach.

A heartfelt thanks also goes to our longtime advisor and mentor, Tim Purdie. We thank him for introducing us to the wonders and frustrations of process management, and for his guidance, encouragement, and support throughout all of our professional endeavors.

Thank you of course to Productivity Press for bringing our work to life and allowing us to write about something that we are both passionate about. We are extremely grateful to our editor, Michael Sinocchi, and our project management team, Stephanie Morkert and Richard Tressider at CRC Press and Suzanna Henry at Deanta Global Publishing Services, for their professional guidance, support, skills, and patience.

To our illustrator and friend, Dustin Duffy. When words were simply not enough, you brought our ideas to life and were able to display their value through remarkable tables, figures, and graphs. Without you, this book would not have been possible.

Finally, we would like to acknowledge with gratitude and love our families, for providing constant support and pushing us to always be better and to never settle for being ordinary. Thank you, Bernie, Fernande, Angie, Jacques, Shannon, and Kalen.

Authors

Tristan Boutros is currently chief operating officer for product, technology and design with *The New York Times*, where he oversees several functions, including product and program management, process improvement, strategic sourcing and vendor management, and enterprise architecture. An award-winning author, speaker, and organizational innovator, he coauthored *The Process Improvement Handbook: A Blueprint for Managing Change and Increasing Organizational Performance* (McGraw-Hill Professional, 2014) and has been written about in several case studies with various outlets. He holds more than 12 professional designations, including his Master Black Belt (MBB), Project Management Professional (PMP), Certified Scrum Professional (CSP), and Master Project Manager (MPM) certifications. A digital and process transformation expert, he specializes in delivering rapid business value using Lean, Agile, and numerous other techniques and methods.

Jennifer Cardella is vice president of strategic program and vendor management for one of the world's largest media and entertainment firms located in New York City. She is a seasoned business leader with an extensive background in program management, process improvement, and business transformation, with key emphasis on product development, cloud computing, operational excellence, and portfolio governance. Jennifer holds more than 10 professional designations, including her Master Black Belt (MBB), Project Management Professional (PMP), Certified Scrum Master (CSM), and Master Project Manager (MPM) certifications. A transformation expert, Jennifer specializes in building high-performing teams and directing the delivery of global business and technology solutions using Lean and Agile methods.

For more information about Tristan or Jennifer's work, professional accolades, or to reach out directly, please visit https://www.linkedin.com/in/tristanboutros or https://www.linkedin.com/in/jennifercardella.
Follow them on Twitter: @TristanBoutros and @JenCardella.

1

Introduction to Process Improvement

Since the mid-twentieth century, the term *process improvement* has come to be accepted as a key concept of management. Today more than ever, organizations worldwide, from manufacturers to hospitals, to banks, to technology companies, are improving operations by adopting process-driven philosophies, mindsets, and methodologies. As a result, demand for process improvement expertise has skyrocketed, and experts have introduced many tools to systematically analyze and improve business, service, and production processes. You've likely heard extensive discussion on business process improvement, process standardization, or process waste in your organization. However, sorting through these various concepts and terms can be frustrating and unsettling. This chapter serves as an introduction to a number of concepts related to process improvement, providing definitions and a foundation to the topic. Understanding the basics of process improvement will help you sharpen your company's competitive edge and position your business for sustained success.

By the end of this chapter, you should be able to

- Define what a process is
- State the objectives of process improvement
- Explain the characteristics of a process
- List the benefits of process improvement
- Identify the steps needed to improve business processes
- Outline common pitfalls with process improvement and how to avoid them
- Describe the various levels of process maturity

WHAT IS A PROCESS?

There are many definitions that exist to describe what a process is, but most commonly it is described as a sequence of linked tasks or activities that, at every stage, consume one or more resources (employee energy, time, infrastructure, machines, and money) to convert inputs (data, material, and parts) into outputs (products, services, or information). Furthermore, processes outline a specific ordering of work activities across time, with a beginning, an end, and clearly defined inputs and outputs, and serve as the fundamental building blocks of all organizations. Everything we do is a process, and in each area or function of an organization there are many processes being executed. These processes interact with other processes, and organizations large and small can be seen as complex networks of interconnecting processes.

An organization's success hinges in large part on how well it carries out its processes, and an effective process is one that produces intended results consistently and efficiently. A simple example that will help illustrate a process in action is to look at the process of ordering a meal at a restaurant. The process activities are as follows:

1. The process starts when a customer places an order.
2. A waiter then takes the order.
3. The waiter places the order with the kitchen.
4. The chef prepares the order.
5. The process ends with the delivery of the meal to the customer.

 A **process** is a sequence of linked tasks or activities which, at every stage, consume one or more resources (employee energy, time, infrastructure, machines, money) to convert inputs (data, material, parts) into outputs (products, services or information).

WHAT ARE THE CHARACTERISTICS OF A PROCESS?

Every organization wants to develop its business and improve the performance of its daily operational work and the quality of its service delivery. Business processes are the operational activities that provide, produce, and deliver its products and services, and every organization consists of employees who perform activities, using a variety of different resources and with varying levels of control. Therefore, it is important to understand the characteristics of a business process before trying to improve one. There are several core elements to a process. A well-defined process contains five core components:

- Resources
- Inputs
- Activities
- Outputs
- Controls

Resources

Process resources are all of the things that a process must routinely have to be able to convert inputs into outputs. Resources may be tangible or intangible, and examples of resources might include

- Tangible: People, a computer, and software
- Intangible: Skills and experience

Inputs

The Inputs of a process are the things that are transformed by the process into an end product or service required by the customer of the process. Inputs may be tangible or intangible, and examples of inputs might include

- Tangible: Written data, parts, and forms
- Intangible: Verbal requests

Activities

Activities in a process can be thought of as the actions that move the inputs through the process to become outputs. Examples of activities in a process include

- Tangible: Measuring, sawing, nailing, painting, and writing
- Intangible: Reading, approving, or submitting

Outputs

The outputs of a process can be products, services, or information and should conform to the specifications agreed in advance with the customer of the process, whether they are internal or external. Outputs can also be tangible or intangible, and examples include

- Tangible: Products
- Intangible: Advice

Controls

Process controls are activities involved in ensuring a process is predictable, stable, and consistently operating at the target level of performance with only normal variation. Process controls may be imposed either externally or internally. For example, customer specifications, legislative requirements, and copyright laws are all externally imposed, whereas internal quality checks and organizational approvals are derived from within the organization.

Process controls are activities involved in ensuring a process is predictable, stable, and consistently operating at the target level of performance with only normal variation.

Processes outline all of the activities an organization engages in, using people, technology, and information to carry out its goals. All processes are made up of some combination of inputs, outputs, and activities, but the level to which people, systems, data, and rules play a role depends on the type of process. Organizations combine these things in pursuit of a business goal and to add value to the customer. There are many ways to accomplish the same goal and many ways that customers perceive value, so there is almost an infinite number of ways to combine inputs, activities, controls, and resources in a business process that achieves a desired output. The trick is to combine the available inputs, resources, and controls in the most efficient and effective manner to satisfy the customer.

Every business process has a goal, has specific inputs and outputs, uses resources, has a number of activities that are performed in some order, creates value of some kind for the customer (either internal or external), and may effect more than one organizational unit.

WHAT ARE THE DIFFERENT TYPES OF PROCESSES?

Everyone in and related to your organization carries out dozens of processes every day. For example, you may go through the same steps each time you generate a report, resolve a customer complaint, complete a contract, or build a new product. Processes can be formal or informal, whereby formal processes are documented and have well-established steps. For example, you might have process maps for receiving and submitting invoices, or for creating new customer accounts. Formal processes are particularly important when there are legal, safety, regulatory, or financial reasons for following particular steps. Informal processes are more likely to be ones that you have created yourself and that possess a fairly narrow focus. For example, you might have your own set of steps for taking meeting minutes, carrying out market research, or keeping track of tasks. You've likely come across the outcomes of inefficient processes as well. Unhappy customers, stressed colleagues, missed deadlines, and increased costs are just some of the problems that dysfunctional processes can create. Every organization has various types of processes that run its business, but each can usually be categorized into one of three process types: business processes, support processes, and management processes.

Business Processes

These are the processes that reflect the unique competencies of the enterprise and serve as the ultimate reason an organization exists. Also known as a process backbone or value chain, business processes are composed of the core value-creating activities of the enterprise and are the processes that are seen and experienced most closely by and create value in the eyes of the customer. They may include front- and back-office activities such as shipping, invoice generation, or order entry. Business processes are customer focused and may include

- Product development
- Marketing and sales
- Installation or support services

Business processes are the primary processes within an enterprise that reflect the core value-creating activities of a company.

Value-creating business processes are usually cross-functional and begin and end with the external customer, spanning multiple organizational components, regions, or departments. While organizations may have hundreds or even thousands of processes, there are very few core business processes in an enterprise.

Support Processes

Support processes exist to sustain the enterprise and support its core process backbone or value chain. Since the support needs of business organizations are similar, these processes tend to be fairly standard and are frequent candidates for business process outsourcing. The customers of support processes are usually internal customers. Support processes often include

- Finance and accounting
- Legal and human resources
- Facilities
- Information technology

Support Processes are the processes that exist to sustain the enterprise and support its core value-creating processes or value chains.

Management Processes

Management processes usually provide direction for an enterprise and exist to govern its operations. They are generally conducted by senior leaders to set organizational goals, develop visions, and deploy strategies, as well as establish and manage performance targets. Typically, these processes help employees to understand the company's strategic goals and objectives, helping to shape the business and support the processes of the company. Management processes usually focus on

- Understanding market opportunities and risks
- Creating strategy, vision, and goals
- Managing resources within an enterprise

Management Processes are the processes in an enterprise which help plan and govern its operations.

While these three categories play meaningfully different roles, they need to be aligned and integrated in order to enable effective performance of the entire company. Effective and sustained process improvement must consider the management and support processes as well as the core business processes, whether they are formally or informally regarded or used. When everyone follows a well-tested set of steps, there is less duplicated effort, there are fewer errors and delays, and staff and customers feel more satisfied.

 Disjointed processes that are not coordinated, managed, or continuously improved can lead to numerous problems, such as

- Customers complaining about poor product quality or bad service
- Colleagues getting frustrated
- Work being duplicated or not done at all
- Cost increases
- Wasted resources and cycles
- Bottlenecks causing operators to miss deadlines or critical service-level agreements

WHAT IS PROCESS IMPROVEMENT?

Now that you know more about what processes are, let's take a deeper look at what is meant by the term *process improvement. Process improvement* refers to making a process more effective, efficient, or transparent. Process improvement is relevant to all areas of a company because processes naturally degrade over time for any number of reasons. But because business processes are generally invisible, process mapping aside, many people don't consciously think about them or realize the impact they have on performance. Instead, when problems crop up, people often look for someone to blame or try to implement a new technology to overcome the problem; however, these solutions don't usually solve the root cause of issues. Instead, most organizational difficulties stem from faulty processes.

An organization that conducts process improvement focuses on proactive problem resolution in order to avoid misdiagnosis of problems, or even operating in crisis management mode when process degradation occurs. Process improvement uses a set of disciplined tools, methods, and techniques that employees can use to enhance their company's operating environment. A common misconception about process improvement is that it focuses mainly on process redesign. In fact, although the ideas underpinning process improvement ultimately originated in manufacturing, they encompass far more than just reengineering.

Fundamentally, process improvement seeks to refine a company's basic systems to meet changing customer needs more effectively. More broadly, it can be classified as a set of basic management principles that focus on delivering value efficiently to the customer, enabling people to lead and contribute to their fullest potential, discovering better ways of working, and connecting strategy, goals, and meaningful purpose. Every time you improve your company's business processes, you generate crucial benefits for your organization in the form of efficiency gains, cost savings, or greater customer loyalty and profitability. Even small improvements to a relatively simple process can pay big dividends for your organization.

 Process Improvement is the act of making any business process or procedure more effective, efficient, or transparent.

WHAT ARE THE BENEFITS OF PROCESS IMPROVEMENT?

Business process improvement provides many benefits to organizations that undertake it, regardless of the process improvement methodology they adopt. The real key to amassing benefits from process improvement efforts is ensuring that the entire organization, including senior leadership, is behind the efforts and understands the reasons for taking on ongoing improvements.

In the short term, process improvement helps organizations decrease costs and increase efficiency. This can mean more revenue and growth for companies, as well as increased speed, organization, and efficiency. In the long run, process improvement helps create competitive advantage by improving organizational agility. Other key objectives and benefits associated with process improvement include the following:

Increased accountability: One of the primary goals of instituting a process improvement program is to provide greater accountability for departmental functions and ensuring deliverables are met. By documenting all business processes and working to optimize each one, a company can achieve a system of checks and balances, minimizing the potential for fraud, errors, or loss, and affirming that all employees are aware of their responsibilities.

Improved reliability: Effective process improvement can enhance the reliability of information and ensure timely dissemination. It is critical for executives to receive accurate information when needed in order to make important and time-sensitive business decisions. When processes are properly documented and monitored, it is easy to locate the necessary information and quickly produce relevant reports.

Simplified regulatory compliance: From complying with labor laws to submitting mandated financial reports, there are numerous local, state, and federal rules and regulations companies must follow. Process improvement practices help organizations keep track of their obligations, and ensure that they are in compliance with applicable standards and legislation. By following clearly outlined processes and staying up-to-date on changing laws, companies can avoid the potentially costly repercussions of noncompliance.

Waste avoidance: Since process improvement involves assigning and tracking resources and performance. There is generally less waste than in companies that do not actively monitor their processes. Organizations that follow best practices will find that they can dramatically reduce waste, enhance efficiency, and ultimately, boost profitability. Continuous monitoring and improvement can help to address future issues as well.

Enhanced safety and security: Process improvement can also help enforce safety and security measures. By documenting processes and mandating full compliance with them, organizations can help ensure the safety of their employees and protect the company from various other threats, including theft of company assets such as physical resources and confidential information.

 The benefits of a structured process improvement program can include any or all of the following:

- Happier customers
- Streamlined operations
- Consistent quality
- Less waste
- Lower costs
- More sales and market share
- Improved communication
- Higher employee morale

WHAT ARE THE CORE VALUES OF PROCESS IMPROVEMENT?

Delivering value efficiently to the customer, enabling people to lead and contribute to their fullest potential, discovering better ways of working, and connecting strategy, goals, and meaningful purpose are all critical components in creating a process improvement mindset. All members of an organization must work together to combat waste and redundancy, while also working to prevent the growing number of errors and missteps plaguing true organizational excellence, such as

- Leaders not willing to develop themselves or change their mindsets, behavior, or style to overtly model the changes they are asking of the organization.
- Not adequately or proactively attending to the emotional side of change, such as not designing actions to minimize negative emotional reactions or not attending to them in constructive ways once they occur.
- Buying leading edge rather than best fit. The latest and greatest technology on the market might be impressive, but it may not be what your business needs.
- Selling process improvement as a way to lower costs. This is a short-sighted approach that curtails human involvement and forces initiatives onto employees instead of creating an ongoing mindset of improvement.
- Misdiagnosing the scope of the organizational change either in magnitude or by initiating only technological- or organizational-based initiatives. This frequently leads to solving only part of a larger systemic problem.
- Not securing management buy-in for process improvement initiatives or failure to link project goals with strategic imperatives. This can lead to wasted cycles or effort focusing on nonissues or priorities.
- Not considering processes in the development of technology or product or system implementation, leading to superficial change and extrapolations of conclusions and wrong decisions based on inductive information.
- Optimizing part of an organization or process at the suboptimization of the whole.

- Running organizational transformation through multiple separate or competing projects instead of aligning all initiatives into one unified effort and ensuring the integration of plans, resources, and timelines.
- Not creating adequate capacity for the organizational change—setting unrealistic, crisis-producing timelines and then laying the change on top of people's already excessive workloads.
- Not adequately addressing the organization's culture as a major force directly influencing the success of organizational change.
- Not adequately engaging and communicating with stakeholders, particularly in the early stages of the organizational change process; relying too heavily on one-way or top-down communication and engaging stakeholders only after an improvement is completed.

In order to assist professionals in combating the common pitfalls associated with making this leap, we created the process improvement manifesto, a listing of core values, originally published in *Process Improvement Handbook: A Blueprint for Managing Change and Increasing Organizational Performance* (McGraw-Hill Professional, 2014), that serve as a guiding approach that can help transform the entire organization, from the front line to the executive suite, allowing it to renew itself continuously for lasting value. The 10 tenants of the manifesto are as follows (Figure 1.1):

Agility: Process improvement values agile and iterative improvement. Because change is inevitable, organizations that wish to continually improve must be able to nimbly adjust to and take advantage of emerging opportunities. This involves focusing on flexible work and planning practices tailored toward incremental improvement.

Quality: Process improvement values quality in all aspects of process improvement, from process creation to retirement, including process, people, and technology changes. Organizations that understand and focus their attention on all facets of quality, from the beginning of transformation initiatives to the end, experience superior results.

Leadership: Process improvement values leadership that is proactive and open to ideas for improving all aspects of an organization. Leaders who communicate and inspire a clear and compelling vision for the future have teams that are more engaged and open to improvement opportunities.

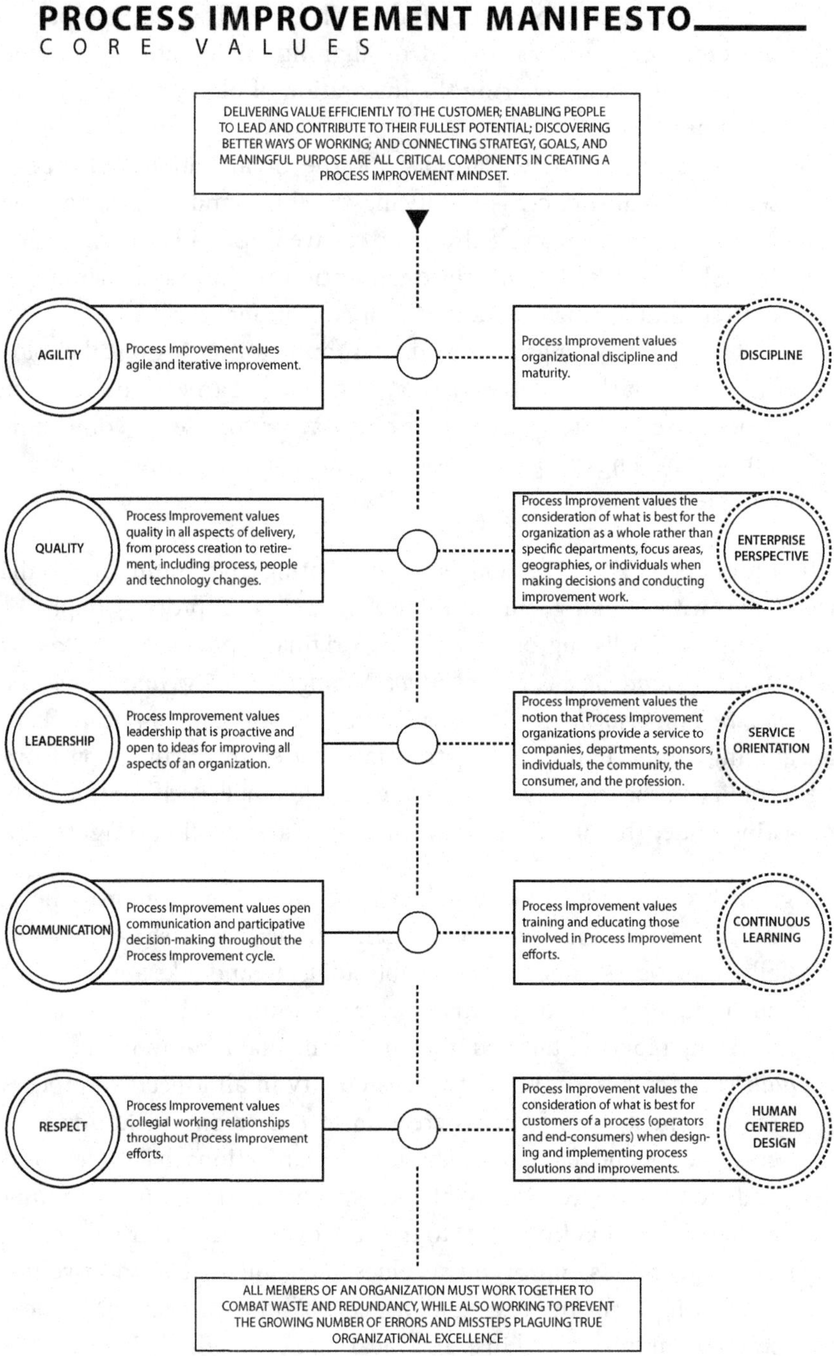

PROCESS IMPROVEMENT MANIFESTO
CORE VALUES

DELIVERING VALUE EFFICIENTLY TO THE CUSTOMER; ENABLING PEOPLE TO LEAD AND CONTRIBUTE TO THEIR FULLEST POTENTIAL; DISCOVERING BETTER WAYS OF WORKING; AND CONNECTING STRATEGY, GOALS, AND MEANINGFUL PURPOSE ARE ALL CRITICAL COMPONENTS IN CREATING A PROCESS IMPROVEMENT MINDSET.

AGILITY — Process Improvement values agile and iterative improvement.

DISCIPLINE — Process Improvement values organizational discipline and maturity.

QUALITY — Process Improvement values quality in all aspects of delivery, from process creation to retirement, including process, people and technology changes.

ENTERPRISE PERSPECTIVE — Process Improvement values the consideration of what is best for the organization as a whole rather than specific departments, focus areas, geographies, or individuals when making decisions and conducting improvement work.

LEADERSHIP — Process Improvement values leadership that is proactive and open to ideas for improving all aspects of an organization.

SERVICE ORIENTATION — Process Improvement values the notion that Process Improvement organizations provide a service to companies, departments, sponsors, individuals, the community, the consumer, and the profession.

COMMUNICATION — Process Improvement values open communication and participative decision-making throughout the Process Improvement cycle.

CONTINUOUS LEARNING — Process Improvement values training and educating those involved in Process Improvement efforts.

RESPECT — Process Improvement values collegial working relationships throughout Process Improvement efforts.

HUMAN CENTERED DESIGN — Process Improvement values the consideration of what is best for customers of a process (operators and end-consumers) when designing and implementing process solutions and improvements.

ALL MEMBERS OF AN ORGANIZATION MUST WORK TOGETHER TO COMBAT WASTE AND REDUNDANCY, WHILE ALSO WORKING TO PREVENT THE GROWING NUMBER OF ERRORS AND MISSTEPS PLAGUING TRUE ORGANIZATIONAL EXCELLENCE

FIGURE 1.1
Process improvement manifesto.

Communication: Process improvement values open communication and participative decision making throughout improvement efforts. An organization that recognizes that everyone has a point of view and should have the opportunity to voice opinions, ideas, and experiences is generally more innovative in its improvement designs.

Respect: Process improvement values collegial working relationships throughout process improvement activities. An organization's success depends increasingly on an engaged workforce that has a safe, trusting, and cooperative work environment. Successful organizations capitalize on the diverse backgrounds, knowledge, skills, creativity, and motivation of their workforce and partners.

Discipline: Process improvement values organizational discipline and maturity. Companies with high organizational discipline and that perform business processes in a standard, repetitive fashion are more competitive and usually leaders in their markets. Ensuring a disciplined approach to all process improvement activities helps ensure thorough and robust solutions are implemented.

Enterprise perspective: Process improvement values the consideration of what is best for the organization as a whole rather than specific departments, focus areas, geographies, or individuals when making decisions and conducting day-to-day work. Ensuring process improvements meet not only the needs of those involved with the activities in question, but also the larger enterprise ensures time and money are not wasted deploying and redeploying solutions.

Service orientation: Process improvement values the notion that process improvement activities provide a service to companies, departments, sponsors, individuals, the community, the consumer, and the profession. This involves doing what is right for the customer in question and endlessly providing expertise for their benefit.

Continuous learning: Process improvement values training and educating those involved in process improvement efforts. The primary objective of training is to provide all personnel, suppliers, and customers with the skills to effectively perform quality process activities, and to build this concept directly into an organization's operations. This practice enables continuous learning within the organization and promotes improvement and process-oriented thinking.

Human-centered design: Process improvement values the consideration of what is best for customers of a process (operators and end consumers) when designing and implementing process solutions and improvements. Ensuring processes are user-friendly for those executing their activities helps maintain positive morale.

Process improvement organizations that embrace these core values are capable of

- Quickly adapting to changing requirements or market factors
- Significantly reducing the risk associated with continuous improvements
- Accelerating the delivery of business value to customers
- Ensuring that value is continually being maximized throughout the continuous improvement process
- Meeting customer requirements faster and more efficiently
- Building innovation and best practices that help reach new maturity levels
- Discovering hidden knowledge and expertise within their workforce
- Improving performance and motivation across all areas of the business

WHAT TRIGGERS PROCESS IMPROVEMENT?

Every organization has its own reasons for adopting a culture of process improvement, and all successful process improvement programs have similar aims and provide similar benefits regardless of the issues that set the program in motion. There are numerous reasons for deciding to implement a process improvement program, such as regulatory issues, introducing industry best practices, rectifying customer satisfaction problems, poor or erratic quality, and discovering excessive costs. Although organizations might consider a process improvement initiative for many reasons, the most common reasons why your organization is likely to consider process improvement engagement fall into seven major categories, as outlined in the following subsections.

Organizational Factors

Organizational factors that may trigger process improvement efforts include

- Difficulty coping with high growth or proactively planning for high growth
- Inheriting additional complexity through mergers and acquisitions
- The need to rationalize processes and systems
- Internal reorganization that brings forth changing roles and responsibilities
- Deciding to change corporate direction to operational excellence, product leadership, or customer intimacy
- Organizational goals and objectives not being met
- Compliance or regulatory requirements

Management Factors

Management factors that may trigger process improvement efforts include

- Lack of reliable or conflicting management information
- The need to provide managers with more control over their processes
- The need to create a culture of high performance
- The need to gain return on investment from the existing legacy investments
- Budget cuts
- A desire to obtain more capacity from existing staff for expansion

Employee Factors

Employee factors that may trigger process improvement efforts include

- High turnover of employees
- Training issues with new employees
- Low employee satisfaction
- A substantial increase in the number of employees
- A desire to increase employee empowerment
- Difficulties with continuous change and growing complexity

Customer, Supplier, and Partner Factors

Customer, supplier, and partner factors that may trigger process improvement efforts include

- Low satisfaction with service
- An increase in the number of customers, suppliers, or partners
- Long lead times to meet requests
- Customer segmentation or tiered service requirements
- The introduction and strict enforcement of service levels
- Major customers, suppliers, or partners requiring a unique process

Product and Service Factors

Product and service factors that may trigger process improvement efforts include

- Long lead times or lack of business agility
- Poor stakeholder engagement or service levels
- Several products or services having their own processes where most activities are common or similar
- New products or services compromising existing product and service elements

Process Factors

Process factors that may trigger process improvement efforts include

- A need for visibility of processes from an end-to-end perspective
- Significant handoffs or gaps in processes
- No documented processes or procedures
- Unclear roles and responsibilities across the organization
- Product or service quality is poor
- The amount of rework is substantial
- Processes change too often or not at all
- Processes are not standardized
- Lack of clear process goals or objectives
- Lack of communication and understanding by workers involved in executing processes

Technology Factors

Technology factors that may trigger process improvement efforts include

- The introduction of new systems
- The purchase of business process management automation tools
- Retirement of aging applications and systems
- Existing application systems overlap
- Introduction of a new IT architectures or technologies
- A view that IT is not delivering to business expectations
- A view that IT costs are out of control or too expensive
- The need to retire duplicate systems

WHAT IS WASTE?

In process improvement terms, waste is any resource consumed by inefficient or nonessential activities, any unwanted material left over from a production process, or any output that has no marketable value. Often referred to as Muda, the idea originated in Japan after World War II, when Taiichi Ohno developed the concept of Lean Manufacturing at Toyota. Process improvement as a general construct is concerned with removing waste from processes to reduce costs, eliminate defects, and increase productivity. There are eight types of waste that can be found and expunged from processes (Figure 1.2):

1. *Transportation*: Moving a product or parts between manufacturing processes adds no value, is expensive, and can cause damage or product deterioration.

    Examples include movement of paperwork, multiple handoffs of information, multiple approval steps, excessive email attachments, and unnecessary cc copies to people who don't really need the information.

2. *Excessive inventory*: Excessive inventory wastes resources through costs of storage and maintenance.

    Examples include purchasing or making things before they are needed, things waiting in an electronic or physical inbox, and mass amounts of unread email.

WASTES

8 T Y P E S   O F   W A S T E

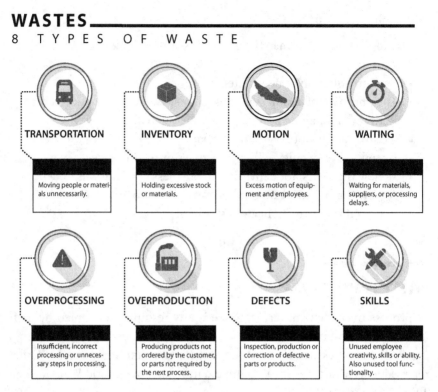

FIGURE 1.2
Eight types of waste.

3. *Unnecessary motion*: Resources are wasted when workers have to bend, reach, or walk long distances to do their jobs. Workplace ergonomics or 5S (sort, straighten, shine, standardize, and sustain) assessments should be conducted to design the most optimal and efficient work environment.

Examples include walking to a copier, printer, or fax; walking between offices; and backtracking back and forth between computer screens.

4. *Waiting*: Processes are ineffective and time is wasted when one process or activity waits to begin while another finishes. The flow of operations should be smooth and continuous.

Examples include slow computer speed, workstation downtime, waiting for approvals, waiting for information from people, and waiting for clarification or correction of work received from upstream processes.

5. *Overprocessing*: Overly elaborate and expensive equipment is wasteful if simpler machinery would work just as well.

    Examples include relying on inspections, checkpoints, reviews, or approvals rather than designing processes to eliminate errors; reentering data into multiple systems or applications; making extra copies; and generating unused reports.

6. *Overproduction*: The manufacturing of products in advance or in excess of demand wastes money, time, and space.

    Examples include printing paperwork that might change before it is needed, processing an order that might change before it is needed, and any processing that is done on a routine schedule regardless of current demand.

7. *Defects*: Product rejects and rework within your processes.

    Examples include data entry errors, other types of order entry or invoice errors, and any error that gets passed downstream only to be returned for correction or clarification.

8. *Underutilization of employee skills*: Employees are typically hired for a specific skill set, but they usually bring other skills and insights to the workplace that should be acknowledged and utilized, yet employees are often underutilized or pigeonholed into specific responsibilities.

    Examples include putting employees in roles that do not exploit their experience, not staffing projects with the right employees, and not allowing open feedback.

 Waste is any resource consumed by inefficient or nonessential activities, any unwanted material left over from a production process, or any output that has no marketable value.

Since the original categories of waste were established, others have been proposed, including

1. Unsafe workplaces and environments: Employee accidents and health issues as a result of unsafe working conditions waste resources, prevent focus, and decrease morale.

2. Lack of information or sharing of information: Research and communication are essential to keep operations working to capacity.

3. Equipment breakdown: Poorly maintained equipment can result in damage and cost resources of both time and money.

4. Environmental: Wasting natural resources also wastes funds and does not promote corporate social responsibility.

Although the eight wastes list was created for manufacturing, the categories can be adapted to apply to most types of workplaces. Figure 1.3 provides some examples of wastes across manufacturing, technology, and service-based industries.

There are two common mnemonics that you can use to help you remember the eight wastes. The first is to ask yourself, "Who is TIM WOODS?"

- Transport
- Inventory
- Motion
- Waiting
- Overprocessing
- Overproduction
- Defects
- Skills

An alternative mnemonic for remembering the traditional eight wastes is WORMPITS:

- Waiting
- Overproduction
- Rejects
- Motion
- Processing
- Inventory
- Transport
- Skills

WHAT IS STANDARDIZATION?

Standardized work is one of the most powerful process improvement concepts. By documenting current best practices, standardized work forms the baseline for continuous improvement. As a process is improved, the new standard of that process becomes the baseline for further improvements. Improving standardized work is a continuous effort and consists of three main components:

8 WASTES EXAMPLES
ALL INDUSTRIES

WASTE	MANUFACTURING	IT AND SERVICE
DEFECTS	Inspection, production or correction of defective parts or products	Any non-conformance or inspection failure requiring rework, review, retest
OVER-PRODUCTION	Producing products not ordered by the customer, or parts not required by the next process	Providing more services than required, requested or can be handled in a process step
WAITING	Waiting for material, suppliers or processing delays	Any time when work is not being performed on a customer request
UNNECESSARY TRANSPORT	Moving material or people unnecessarily	Non-value added processing; movement of files, data or customer request
EXCESS INVENTORY	Holding excessive stock, or raw materials	Work in process and excessive office infrastructure and materials
UNNECESSARY MOTION	Excess motion of equipment or employees (searching, waking, stacking, filing)	Movement to transport information or data or compensating for inefficient processes
OVER-PROCESSING	Inefficient, incorrect processing or unecessary steps in production	Any effory that adds no value to the product, service or customer
NON-UTILIZED TALENTS	Unused employee creativity, skills or ability	Unused employee creativity, skills or ability. Also unused tool functionality.

FIGURE 1.3
Eight examples of waste across all industries.

1. *Takt time*, which is the rate at which products must be made or services rendered in a process to meet customer demand
2. *Work in process (WIP)*, which is the work sequence and volume in which an operator performs tasks within takt time
3. *Standard inventory*, which is the inventory required to keep the process operating smoothly

Standardization is an important part of process improvement because it maximizes efficiency and minimizes waste. Using standard forms or documents ensures that workers always know where to find the information they need to do their jobs, without wasting time or energy. Standard tools and equipment ensure that workers know how to do their jobs without requiring training as they move between workstations, facilities, or tasks. The goal of standardization is to create efficiencies while removing communication issues and opportunities for error. Some examples of standardization include

- Creating an enterprise-wide glossary to reduce interdepartmental communication problems
- Using templates to speed up documentation processes
- Creating templates within a factory environment so that all parts are the same and it's easy to convert between parts or sizes
- Using scripts in call centers to align the message that is provided to customers

Standardized work is also advantageous to workers themselves. If chosen with care and concern for employees, standards ensure that each task in the workplace is achievable and sustainable, as well as safe, from both a risk and a compliance point of view. In other words, standardized work is a precursor to excellence, a catalyst for worker satisfaction, and a critical stepping-stone for continuous process improvement. Using a seven-step framework called the standardization work wheel, originally created by Booz & Company, companies can implement standardization in the workplace for all types of employees in all types of industries (Figure 1.4).

1. *Taking inventory*: Use tools like process mapping to determine which aspects of production must be standardized. Process mapping can help define the material and information flows that most impact

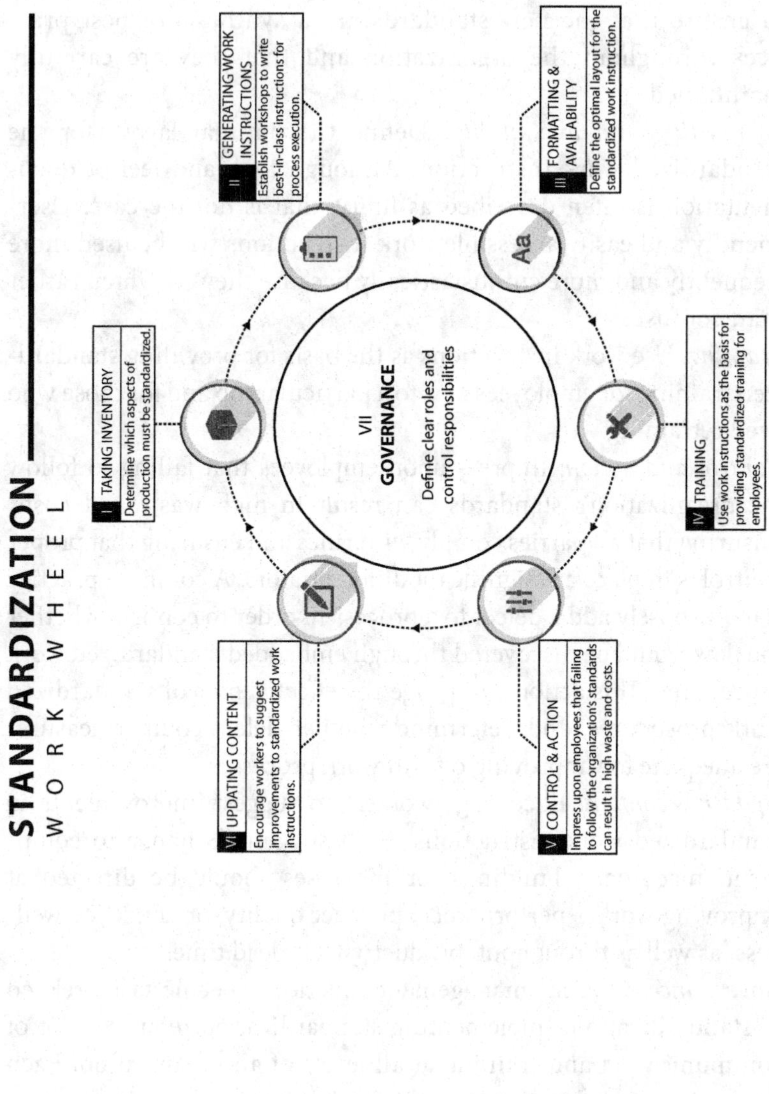

STANDARDIZATION
W O R K   W H E E L

I TAKING INVENTORY
Determine which aspects of production must be standardized.

II GENERATING WORK INSTRUCTIONS
Establish workshops to write best-in-class instructions for process execution.

III FORMATTING & AVAILABILITY
Define the optimal layout for the standardized work instruction.

IV TRAINING
Use work instructions as the basis for providing standardized training for employees.

V CONTROL & ACTION
Impress upon employees that failing to follow the organization's standards can result in high waste and costs.

VI UPDATING CONTENT
Encourage workers to suggest improvements to standardized work instructions.

VII GOVERNANCE
Define clear roles and control responsibilities

FIGURE 1.4
Standardization work wheel.

quality, lead time, and cycle time, and can focus the organization on the critical work instructions that would most benefit from standardization. It is a way of learning what is really going on in your company's operations.

2. *Generating work instructions*: Establish workshops to write best-in-class instructions for process execution. These sessions should be multifunctional, involving employees from all needed areas of operations, engineering, quality control, or other departments to ensure that the new standards are a synthesis of best practices throughout the organization and that they are carefully maintained.

3. *Formatting and availability*: Define the optimal layout for the standardized work instruction. Although look and feel of documentation is often described as fluffy, that is not the case. User-friendly and easily accessible work instructions will be used more frequently and more enthusiastically because they enlighten rather than confuse.

4. *Training*: Use work instructions as the basis for providing standardized training for employees new to a particular job and for those who need retraining.

5. *Control and action*: Impress upon employees that failing to follow the organization's standards can result in high waste and costs. Ensuring that all parties comply with rules and ensuring that proper control is in place are significant differentiators. A common practice is to purposely add a defect to a process in order to confirm whether the flaw would be discovered through embedded standardized work procedures. This action can gauge the effectiveness of standardized work procedures, and determine whether defect countermeasures are adequate for improving overall work processes.

6. *Updating content*: Encourage workers to suggest improvements to standardized work instructions. Each suggested change to equipment, machinery, buildings, or processes should be directed at improving worker performance, product quality, or employee wellness, as well as throughput, productivity, or lead time.

7. *Governance*: Give all management functions specific tasks related to standardization. Implementing standardization requires a lot of communication and training at all levels of an organization. Each person in the corporate pyramid has a job to do in making sure that standardization is established in a sustainable way.

Standardization is the formulation and implementation of guidelines, rules, and specifications for common and repeated use, aimed at achieving optimum efficiency or uniformity in a process, organization, or system.

These seven steps begin the journey toward adherence to standards and the development of a foundation for successful process improvement.

WHAT IS PROCESS MATURITY?

Process maturity is an indication of how close a process or organization is to being complete and capable of continual improvement through qualitative measures and feedback. For an organization to be mature, its processes have to be complete and useful, automated where applicable, reliable in information, and continuously improved. However, most businesses have a limited understanding of end-to-end business processes, and if any understanding exists, it is often within disparate groups across the organization. It's rare to find an organization that has linked together its scattered process competencies to support a comprehensive process excellence strategy. Organizations that want to achieve process excellence continually evaluate their processes and operational components, including data quality, health of culture, technologies, and policies and controls, while looking for ways to increase efficiency, improve productivity, and eliminate waste. Organizations seeking process excellence usually measure themselves against a five-stage maturity model to guide them toward process excellence.

The five stages of process maturity are as follows:

- *Level 1—Informal (ad hoc)*: Several undocumented process with no real structure or organization in place, and employees usually achieve success through individual heroics.
- *Level 2—Documented (repeatable)*: Some processes are organized and documented with potentially repeatable results. Best practices are starting to emerge and measurements are being thought about.
- *Level 3—Integrated (defined)*: Most processes are defined and confirmed as a standard business process. Process improvement practices are beginning to emerge and projects to improve processes have started.

- *Level 4—Managed (cross-functional)*: Processes are managed using defined metrics and are beginning to be articulated in cross-functional terms. Cultural and company structures and tools are in place to ensure process improvement occurs and is strategically aligned.
- *Level 5—Optimized (continuous improvement)*: Process management includes repeated attempts to optimize for continuous improvement. Processes are cross-functionally integrated, and process improvement is built into all components of the organization.

 Process Maturity is a concept used to assess an organization against a scale of five process maturity levels. Each level ranks the organization according to its standardization of processes in the area being assessed.

Figure 1.5 provides a description of the typical triggers that herald an organization's transition from one phase to another, such as the business characteristics for each phase and the needed competencies.

A way to determine how well the processes of your organization can reliably and sustainably be reproduced is to conduct a process maturity assessment. Maturity assessments provide

- A basis for setting as-is and to-be positions
- Support for gap analysis to define what needs to be done to achieve a certain level
- Support for benchmark comparison with other organizations
- A standard set of practices to compare against
- A basis for determining where you are on the maturity scale
- A baseline measurement of maturity to compare against at some point in the future
- An overview on which areas need the most focus, from both a process perspective and an organizational perspective

Figure 1.6 outlines a basic survey to help you determine the maturity of your organization's processes and initiatives in an objective way. Complete the assessment and receive a set of scores indicating your process maturity across four dimensions that are key to deriving value from process improvement.

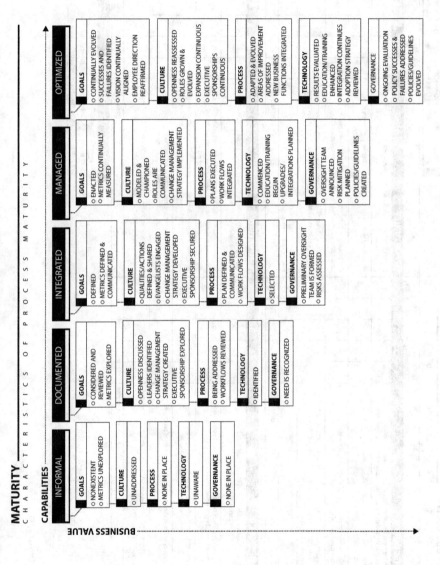

FIGURE 1.5

Process maturity characteristics.

ASSESSMENT
PROCESS EXCELLENCE SURVEY

INDICATE THE EXTENT TO WHICH YOU BELIEVE THE STATEMENT DESCRIBES YOUR COMPANY'S PROCESS EXCELLENCE JOURNEY.

DIRECTION	NOT AT ALL DESCRIPTIVE 1	2	3	4	VERY DESCRIPTIVE 5
We have a process excellence vision that we frequently communicate and that is well understood by our employees.					
We have established strategies and objectives to support our process excellence vision.					
We have measures of process excellence to promote alignment across organizational units.					
Our employees have a common understanding of the specific behaviors that are needed to demonstrate and deliver our process excellence priorities.					
We "stay the course" in our process excellence priorities.					
TOTAL SCORE					

OPPORTUNITY	NOT AT ALL DESCRIPTIVE 1	2	3	4	VERY DESCRIPTIVE 5
We have the necessary resources to execute our process excellence priorities.					
We actively work to remove barriers to process performance.					
Our process owners/teams meet regularly to assess process performance and initiate improvement opportunities.					
Our teams and clients have the necessary authority to review our work processes to enhance the delivery of value to our customers.					
Our internal clients readily seek out opportunities to participate in process improvement efforts.					
TOTAL SCORE					

COMPETENCE	NOT AT ALL DESCRIPTIVE 1	2	3	4	VERY DESCRIPTIVE 5
We have adequate expert resources proficient in process improvement tools and methodologies.					
Our process owners effectively manage cross-functional process performance and improvement priorities.					
Line managers accept ownership for initiating and sustaining process improvement and excellence initiatives.					
Our employees have the necessary skills to improve processes.					
Our employees understand how we deliver value to customers and the operational drivers of our performance.					
TOTAL SCORE					

MOTIVATION	NOT AT ALL DESCRIPTIVE 1	2	3	4	VERY DESCRIPTIVE 5
We actively reinforce our employees and process teams in a timely manner for improvement.					
We consistently role-model process management leadership behaviors that demonstrate collaboration, cross-functional alignment, and data-based decision making.					
We have created a culture where our employees "want to" rather than "have to" contribute to our process excellence vision and strategies					
Our culture emphasizes frequent, candid feedback on how the company, the team, and individuals are performing.					
Our formal policies and practices are consistent with the behaviors and process excellence culture we envision.					
TOTAL SCORE					

SCORING KEY

<55 points	BELOW AVERAGE (gaps exist, needs improvement)
55–71 points	AVERAGE (on par with other leaders)
>71 points	HIGH (ahead of other leaders - doing the "right" things)

FIGURE 1.6
Process maturity survey.

WHAT ARE THE PHASES OF PROCESS IMPROVEMENT?

Process improvement offers crucial benefits to any team or organization, but to generate those benefits, you need to take a structured approach to your project efforts. Every process improvement methodology has its own set of tools and phases, but most improvement projects follow the same general outline. Not only do most accepted process improvement methodologies put the customer at the center of the effort, but also they all have similar methods for achieving the goals. Commonalities include measuring results and trying additional countermeasures to ensure continuous improvement. All assume that process improvement is a journey that continues throughout the life of the organization rather than a destination that is reached and the journey ends. Common phases of process improvement include planning, analyzing, designing, implementing, and continuously improving:

Planning: During the planning phase, most methodologies suggest identifying and clarifying the issue or challenge clearly and succinctly. During the planning phase, activities might include chartering a team to work on the project, identifying the problem, and presenting the project to a sponsor or executive team for approval or endorsement. Teams will also have to begin measuring applicable metrics and come up with a definition of what success is going to look like. Factors to be considered in this phase include the following.

Analyzing: Analyzing the current state by documenting the as-is process, deciding on the appropriate metrics and goals, and taking baseline measurements occurs in the analysis phase. Teams continue to gather information during the analyze phase, which might include one or more process maps. They also analyze data, come up with possible root causes for the problem, and validate those causes. Toward the end of the analyze phase, teams brainstorm solutions and decide which solutions they will move forward with.

Designing: During the design phase, the team focuses on identifying as many countermeasures as possible to reach the intended goals of the improvement project. They prioritize the countermeasures based on perceived impact, and design a to-be process that they believe will help meet the goals of the organization. During design phases, teams design new processes or products that will solve the problem or improve the situation. In many projects, this might mean developing new technical solutions.

Implementing: At this point, the change is documented and the organization begins using the new process. The team measures the results and compares them to baseline results or other benchmarks. Changes are often tested to ensure that processes react as expected to changes and new problems and risks are not created. After teams confirm that implemented solutions are working as planned, they put controls in place to ensure ongoing performance and quality. Processes are then transitioned back to the needed owners and participants.

Continuously improving: The job of business process improvement does not stop after your first improvement effort. It is the ongoing responsibility of teams and process operators to ensure that processes are continually improved. Business processes must be monitored and analyzed continually to discover any opportunities for improvement. It is a journey toward excellence, and all of you and those involved in ongoing operations should continually be looking for new and better ways of working.

 Several other formal process improvement methodologies and standards exist in the market today, including Six Sigma, Lean, Lean Six Sigma, Rummler-Brache, business process reengineering (BPR), ISO 9000, total quality management (TQM), and statistical process control (SPC).

As befits continuous improvement efforts, the process may cycle back to step 1, or the team may elect to adopt another one of the possible improvements identified in the first cycle. It's important to give the new process time to stabilize and to collect metrics before introducing the next variable, or the results may not be verifiable. Improvement is infinite and teams should never stop looking for the next opportunity to increase profit, reduce errors, or create better customer satisfaction. Once one improvement is in the continuous improvement phase, teams should move on to identify the next problem or opportunity.

 In its simplest form, there are six common steps needed to improve a business process:

1. Identify the process to be improved and scope the improvement effort.
2. Map and analyze the process.

3. Redesign the process.
4. Test and implement the process.
5. Continually improve the process.

WHERE DO I START?

One of the most frequently asked questions we get from people in organizations that see the value of process improvement practices and are eager to begin reaping its benefits is "Where should we start?" The answer to this question depends on many factors, but ideally, an organization looking to transform and improve itself already has a defined purpose, consensus around its strategic direction, clearly defined business goals, and alignment around several improvement opportunities that are needed to meet or exceed its goals. If not, leaders and employees alike will want to start by gathering information about the organization in order to identify the biggest areas for improvement or opportunity.

Other tips for developing a process-oriented culture and beginning process improvement efforts include

1. *Clearly defining what success looks like:* Look across the entire organization and define what success looks like for all areas of the business.
2. *Defining your preferred culture:* In the same way that leaders shape and communicate a vision, they also need to spell out a picture of the culture they are striving for and expectations of behaviors.
3. *Setting stretch targets:* Employees tend to rise to the standard set for them. The more you expect, the more they will achieve. But there is a fine line between good stretch targets, which can energize an organization, and bad ones, which can stifle morale.
4. *Connecting the dots:* Most employees want to be a part of a compelling future and want to know what is most important at work and what excellence looks like. For targets to be meaningful and effective in motivating employees, they must be tied to larger organizational ambitions.
5. *Developing a sense of ownership:* When individuals understand the boundaries in which they can operate, as well as where the company wants to go, they feel empowered with a freedom to decide and act, and most often make the right choices.

6. *Improving transparency:* By sharing information with employees, you can increase employees' sense of ownership. Outlining where process or performance deficiencies exist, and being transparent about improvement plans, helps create a sense of urgency and a united front.

7. *Increasing employee engagement:* Employees who are engaged put their heart and soul into their job and have the energy and excitement to give more than is required of the job. Engaged employees are committed and loyal to the organization.

8. *Encourage participation:* Gathering feedback and ensuring proper channels exist to discuss concerns while creating an openness to cross-training employees are needed to further encourage employee involvement and promote specific process improvement activities.

9. *Training and education:* Focused training of all staff and team members is required for understanding what is and what is not the essence of process improvement. Team leaders should be trained to understand continuous improvement in an organizational context, as well as learning about the necessity of impartial evaluation and improving participation.

10. *Process improvement:* After training is completed, true process improvement can begin, where all employees begin to see their work in a new light and openly begin discussing problems, identifying root causes, and proposing solutions.

11. *Quality improvement:* Once process improvements are underway, employees should continue to focus on long-term implications, widespread applications, and alignment with organizational objectives and planning objectives.

12. *Celebrate:* Lastly, do remember to celebrate milestones once they have been reached. Taking the time to celebrate is important because it acknowledges people's hard work, boosts morale, and keeps up the momentum.

CLOSING REMARKS

Establishing process improvement behaviors within your organization is critical to its survival, and you and your team can create enormous value for your company by adopting a process mindset. When you and your colleagues demonstrate process-oriented thinking, it means you regularly think about how to improve the way your groups operate. You seek to understand the quality of your organization's processes and seek to discover and correct weak points. You cultivate a process mindset in your team by helping team members understand and articulate the many processes they take part in, and encourage them to constantly look for ways to improve those processes.

Despite its apparent simplicity, process improvement isn't always easy. It can be difficult to get people to acknowledge shortcomings in their current ways of working. It can be difficult to get busy technical people to spend time learning and trying new techniques. It can be difficult to get managers interested in future strategic benefits when they have looming deadlines. Lastly, it's very difficult to change the culture of an organization. The reward at the end of this adventure, though, is quite satisfying and can ultimately lead to greater efficiency, higher customer satisfaction, and reduced errors within your firm.

2

Process Mapping

Successful process improvement efforts must begin with a solid foundation. One practice that can ensure a firm foundation is the act of process mapping. Whether processes are efficient or inefficient, effective or ineffective, boring or exciting, they serve as the foundation required for all companies to function and improve. Mapping business processes is a critical exercise required for any company that wishes to automate, reorganize personnel, improve performance, merge, acquire or sell a business, meet regulatory requirements, or realize accelerated growth. The reason many organizations fail to sufficiently address and document their business processes is because it's believed that everyone within the organization already understands these processes. But seldom do all personnel have a consistent understanding of any one process or how it affects various other parts of the organization. A key element of all process improvement is to define the sequence of activities undertaken, as a necessary step prior to any development of new improvements or changes. While anyone can create a process map, using process mapping as a tool for process improvement or process design can mean depicting complex processes. Creating an accurate, understandable diagram of such processes takes specific skills and experience. This chapter aims to provide guidance and the basic principles of process mapping, while also describing various types of process maps. Understanding the basics of process mapping will help you better invest the time and money necessary to continually update business process documentation.

By the end of this chapter, you should be able to

- Define what process mapping is
- State the objectives of process mapping
- List the benefits of process mapping

- Explain the characteristics of a process map
- Identify the various types of process maps
- Explain the steps needed to create process maps

WHAT IS PROCESS MAPPING?

If someone asked you if your business processes were documented, would you know how to answer? If your answer is that you wouldn't know where to look or that the processes were stored in an out-of-date repository, or that you just weren't sure, your organization is probably not collaborating well regarding its processes. There are two indisputable truths about processes:

1. They are at the core of business operations and every organization runs on them.
2. Business workers are the real experts about how processes run and how they can be improved in the future.

Process mapping is the step-by-step description of the actions taken by workers as they use a specific set of inputs to produce a defined set of outputs. The resulting process maps depict the inputs, the performers, the sequence of actions the performers take, and the outputs of a work process, usually combining both words and simple graphics. The maps may also include the elapsed time required to perform each step, systems the performers use, conditions of work, business rules, and several other elements. Ultimately, process mapping is an exercise to identify all the steps and decisions in a process in diagrammatic form that

- Displays the various tasks and activities contained within the process
- Describes the flow of materials, information, and documents
- Shows that the tasks transform inputs into outputs
- Indicates the decisions that need to be made throughout the process
- Demonstrates the essential interrelationships and interdependencies between process steps
- Enables you to examine processes thoroughly and develop improvements

Depending on the scope of the process in question, a process map may focus on a department, a business unit, a division, a work group, or even an individual performer. If the process involves a complex area such as a cross-functional business unit, a series of maps may be produced beginning at the highest level of detail, for example, the business unit and how it's connected to other areas, and then proceeding to lower levels, such as articulating the activities being conducted within each division or work group.

Process mapping is typically conducted by a facilitator working with a small group of performers who are especially knowledgeable about the process or the techniques needed to conduct process improvements. This group often includes the process owner, subject matter experts or top performers, and representatives of each work group that participate in the process. The facilitator prompts the group to define the departments involved, the process inputs and tasks, the sequence of tasks, the resulting outputs, and any other elements of importance. This can be done using a traditional paper-and-pen method, such as Post-its on a wall, where activities are arranged and rearranged in sequence until stakeholders are satisfied that the process is accurately and comprehensively portrayed. Another approach is to enter each process element into a software program that automatically organizes the information into a process map.

 Process Mapping is a pictorial, step-by-step description of the actions taken by workers as they execute processes.

WHAT ARE THE BENEFITS OF PROCESS MAPPING?

One of the best ways to analyze a process is to make it visible. Process mapping offers an outlet for capturing, analyzing, and improving the way your business works by providing a single format for all your business processes. As you document your processes, you can see and analyze all the details behind each activity. For example, who performs the task? Who is the business owner? How long does it take? What resources are used throughout? What value does it create? Process mapping also makes it easier for other stakeholders to add their knowledge and modify the processes as needed. Essentially, you're creating a living, breathing document that can easily be updated as the team captures more and more detail about how your organization does business.

In doing so, process mapping creates a shared understanding and overview of what is involved in a process. One of the largest benefits of a process map is that it delivers a graphical representation of a complex or abstract idea. Because everyone learns and ingests information differently, some individuals interact better with a picture than they would with a written or spoken narrative. Invoking a process map in a meeting, presentation, or a training class can help ensure everyone is getting the message and is on the same page.

It has been estimated that people working in organizations can waste about a third of their time by redoing things that are incorrect, chasing things without result, querying incomplete instructions, or doing other people's jobs. As it provides an overall view of the entire business structure, a process map can be understood as an outline for developing multiple management viewpoints and allows process improvement to be conducted on a clear, comprehensible, and customer-oriented basis.

There are many benefits to mapping organizational processes:

- Process mapping helps organizations highlight the interactions of individuals or work groups and how the work of one entity is affected by the work of another.
- Process mapping can be adapted to studying the work of entire organizations or business units, functions, work groups, or individuals.
- Process mapping requires a small investment of time and employee involvement in order to collect a large amount of valuable data and helps identify quick-win improvement opportunities.
- Process maps can also serve as effective educational and communication tools.
- Process mapping provides straightforward data that require little or no interpretation.
- Process improvement, process redesign, and process reengineering efforts depend in large part on process maps to help reveal opportunities to improve or standardize processes.
- Process maps assist with establishing and documenting best practices.
- Mapping helps organizations plan objectives, assumptions, and overall values.

- Mapping exercises help prepare your organization to make the transition into system requirements analysis because they describe how the functions would interact with a system to complete an activity step.
- Business or process analysts can use process maps to structure business user requirements in order to be able to validate them and document them for use by others.
- Process mapping also helps articulate the types of information systems or applications used in a process, and is useful when projects involve integrating enterprise applications with current legacy and custom applications.
- Mapping business activities helps to document contingency, disaster recovery, and business continuity plans.
- Maps help teams stay focused on factual details, not on someone's opinion.
- Process maps promote and foster a process-centric attitude in the workplace and get people to think together toward a common goal in a structured way.
- Maps ensure effective integration of business operation during acquisitions, mergers, or sales, including formation of common business practices and understanding of system platforms.

Although there are many benefits associated with process mapping, there are also a few drawbacks:

- It requires a high level of facilitation skill to guide a group through the process mapping exercise. However, individual interviews can be used to gather information from parties with a simple review upon completion.
- Process mapping is typically based on input from a small group of employees. Wider input can be achieved by circulating any draft maps to larger groups for review and feedback.
- As with most data collection methods, the quality of the data collected depends heavily on the accuracy of the information provided by participating employees.
- Individuals who do not like working with detail can find it very difficult to sit for the time usually required to create a process map.
- Unless proper maintenance and governance practices are in place, documentation can become stale.

WHAT IS THE DIFFERENCE BETWEEN PROCESS MAPPING AND PROCESS MODELING?

Sometimes the terms *business process mapping* and *business process modeling* are used interchangeably to refer to documenting how a business operates and how inputs and outputs flow through a system. Understanding the difference between process mapping and process modeling is important when leading improvement projects.

Process mapping is used to identify the activities of a process and who is responsible for executing each task. Business process modeling also allows teams to create pictures of processes within an organization, but it goes one step further by incorporating ideas such as economics, relationships, data, and business rules, and embeds these added layers into the visual diagram to create an all-encompassing profile. Modeling allows you to go deeper into the relationships among processes and their components and includes visual indicators that communicate relationships to other aspects of the enterprise, such as how work products are input and output from activities, what is manual and what is automated, how processes are supported by human or system resources, if there are controls or measurements in place, and what data elements are used. In essence, whereas process mapping is a static artifact, process models are a more dynamic and intelligent way of diagramming. Process models are usually created using an interface or software program that automatically manages many of the drawing tasks. Time-savers like placing shapes quickly, reusing model objects in diagrams, and dragging and dropping previously created activities, subprocesses, and other objects help capture processes quickly all while ensuring consistency.

Process maps put the microscope on procedures and roles; modeling allows the teams to review the outcomes and provide some assistance with testing, by incorporating more data and a dynamic approach to the information. In essence, business process mapping is a tool focused on documentation. It shows how work is done—not necessarily how it should be done or how changes to that process affect other relationships in the enterprise. Process models are much more than connected activities on a page and assist with deeper in-depth analysis and optimizing inefficiencies and bottlenecks.

Overall, the skills required to map or model processes are similar, and both approaches provide several of the same benefits, such as increasing control and efficiency. Process modeling is, however, in many ways a richer image of the business because it provides additional depth that mapping does not—if maps are two-dimensional images, models are their three-dimensional counterpart. Regardless of the tool or approach, visualizing is one of the most important factors in understanding and seeing work in a new light. By modeling your processes in a visual way, you are increasing the potential for success that your organization will understand its processes and have a foundation for analyzing and improving them and effectively communicating change to all that are affected. Figure 2.1 further outlines some of the key differences between process mapping and modeling.

 Process modeling is the act of creating pictures of processes within an organization, similar to process mapping, but also incorporating ideas such as economics, relationships, data as well as business rules, and embedding these added layers into the visual diagram to create an all encompassing process profile.

WHAT ARE THE DIFFERENT TYPES OF PROCESS MAPS?

When we talk about process mapping, many people default to the idea of a flowchart. Flowcharts are extremely useful tools in both process improvement and training, but they are only one of several options available to diagram a process. This section covers a variety of process map types and describes why you would use each type, as well as how to create and interpret the various diagrams.

Stakeholder Map

Stakeholder mapping is a collaborative process of research, debate, and discussion that draws from multiple viewpoints to determine a key list of stakeholders across an entire stakeholder spectrum. Stakeholders include those with an interest in a process or improvement project, and often, these are the individuals or groups who benefit in some way from the process. In its simplest form, stakeholder mapping is a graphical representation of a stakeholder analysis used to understand the internal and external stakeholders, individuals, companies, institutions a process relates to, and what expectations they hold on the process or improvement effort, thus

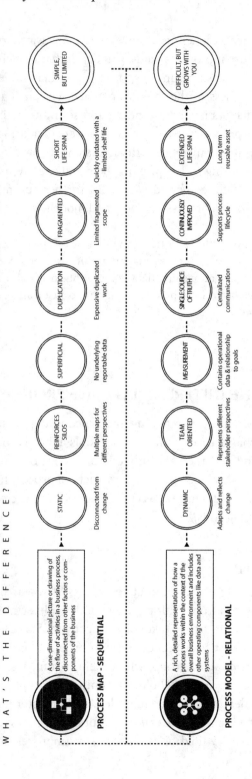

PROCESS MAP VS. PROCESS MODEL
WHAT'S THE DIFFERENCE?

PROCESS MAP - SEQUENTIAL

A one-dimensional picture or drawing of the flow of activities in a business process, disconnected from other factors or components of the business

STATIC — Disconnected from change

REINFORCES SILOS — Multiple maps for different perspectives

SUPERFICIAL — No underlying reportable data

DUPLICATION — Expensive duplicated work

FRAGMENTED — Limited fragmented scope

SHORT LIFE SPAN — Quickly outdated with a limited shelf life

SIMPLE, BUT LIMITED

PROCESS MODEL - RELATIONAL

A rich, detailed representation of how a process works within the context of the overall business environment and includes other operating components like data and systems

DYNAMIC — Adapts and reflects change

TEAM ORIENTED — Represents different stakeholder perspectives

MEASUREMENT — Contains operational data & relationship to goals

SINGLE SOURCE OF TRUTH — Centralized communication

CONTINUOUSLY IMPROVED — Supports process lifecycle

EXTENDED LIFE SPAN — Long term reusable asset

DIFFICULT, BUT GROWS WITH YOU

FIGURE 2.1

Process mapping vs. process modeling.

dictating their likely position or feeling. The process of stakeholder mapping is as important as the result, and the quality of the process depends heavily on the knowledge of the people participating.

Creating a Stakeholder Map

A stakeholder map can become a complex exercise depending on how detailed your map needs to be, but for this purpose, we will simplify the approach and plot stakeholders in a simple map and subsequent grid. The steps in creating a stakeholder map include

1. Begin identifying the internal and external stakeholders related to the process or process improvement project. This is typically done via a brainstorming session. Ensure that the group understands the overall objective and scope of the effort, and ensure your stakeholders are properly categorized around the business unit or process in question. Use arrows or lines to visually link stakeholders to your effort and their proper categories (see Figure 2.2).

2. Allow the team to assess the individuals based on two scales. The first scale rates each stakeholder on interest and support. The second rates power and influence. Again, this is done via a brainstorming session or even asking individuals and partners directly. You can rank stakeholders in relation to each other, but it is usually more accurate to rate each person independently using a numeric scale, with 0 being no interest or influence and 10 being ultimate interest or influence.

3. Once you've identified and ranked the stakeholders, you must plot them according to those ratings. Many stakeholder grids use larger fonts to indicate the strength of support. Others might utilize color to identify and differentiate the positions of the stakeholders; for example, green signifies positive stakeholders, yellow neutral, and red negative. In many cases, the grid itself depicts the key groups of stakeholders requiring management well enough (Figure 2.3).

 A **stakeholder map** is a process and visual tool used in project management and, in particular, stakeholder analysis to clarify and categorize the various stakeholders by drawing pictures of what the stakeholder groups are, which interests they represent, the amount of power they possess, and whether they represent inhibiting or supporting factors for the organization or project to realize its objectives.

STAKEHOLDER BRAINSTORMING_____
W H O   H A S   I N T E R E S T ?

> Brainstorming all possible interested parties and stakeholders help prioritize and ensure proper involvement and communication

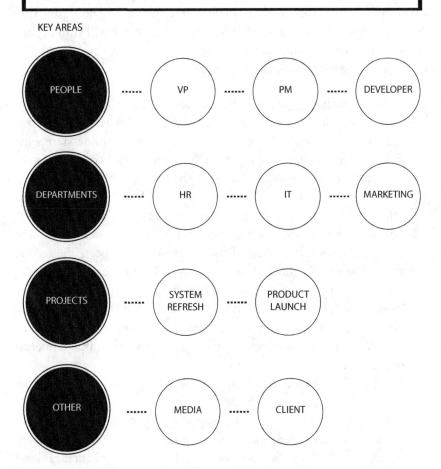

KEY AREAS

FIGURE 2.2
Stakeholder brainstorming. VP, vice president; PM, project manager; HR, human resources; IT, information technology.

Key Features

Among the key features is a mapping of those with interest in a project or process, as well as a subsequent grid ranked and organized appropriately. Possible stakeholders include

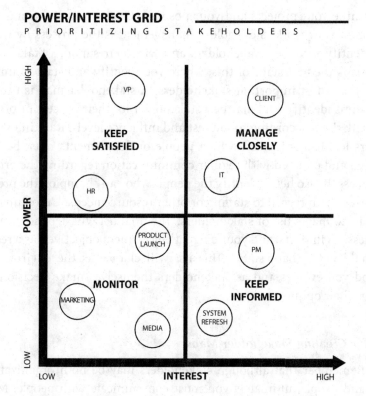

FIGURE 2.3
Stakeholder prioritization grid.

- Owners (investors or shareholders)
- Industry (outside agencies that rate or review suppliers or competitors)
- Community (residents, schools, or special interest groups)
- Customers (direct or indirect)
- Employees (current or potential)
- Government (public authorities or regulators)
- Thought leaders

How to Interpret a Stakeholder Map

Top-ranked or larger stakeholders are those with more influence or needs related to the project or process.

Why Use a Stakeholder Map?

As the work you do and the projects you run become more important, you will affect more and more people. Some of these people have the power to undermine your projects and your position. Others may be strong supporters of your work. Stakeholder management is the process by which you identify your key stakeholders and win their support. Stakeholder analysis is the first stage of this, where you identify and start to understand your most important stakeholders. A stakeholder map is used to help teams identify who may be a stakeholder for their process or project and rank them according to interest and influence levels. Ranking stakeholders lets teams identify which people or departments must be kept satisfied and updated with regular communication regarding the project or process. It also helps identify the people who can champion the project or process with regard to staffing or other resource needs. Unfortunately, there is no magic list of stakeholders. The final list will depend on your business, its impacts, and your current engagement objectives; as a result, it should not remain static. This list will change as the environment around you evolves and as stakeholders themselves make decisions or change their opinions.

Tips for Creating Stakeholder Maps

- Remember that although stakeholders may be both organizations and people, ultimately you must communicate with people. Make sure that you identify the correct individual stakeholders within a stakeholder organization.
- Try not to include too many or too little stakeholders. Too few often means important stakeholders that truly have a stake in the effort or who can influence it accordingly are overlooked. Too many can lead to the artifact itself becoming unusable or inefficient and the impact of true support becoming diluted.
- Don't be afraid to consult stakeholders if you are uncertain about their position or future plans.

Relationship Map

A process relationship map shows dependencies between key processes by using labeled arrows to depict the inputs and outputs flowing between processes across an organization, along with its suppliers and customers. A relationship map helps you view work at a high level and thus does not explicitly articulate work activities. Rather, it shows the input and output connections among selected parts of the organization or the whole enterprise. Building this model usually requires the creation of a process inventory and a process profile for each process in order to ensure completeness. Figure 2.4 is an example of a relationship map.

How to Create a Relationship Map

The steps in creating a stakeholder map include

1. Complete a process inventory for the major processes within a specified organization (an entire enterprise, a profit center, a function, a location, etc.). A process inventory is a list of all of the key processes and their major components. Key features include
   a. Suppliers
   b. Process
   c. Customers
2. Describe the purpose of the process and its type (management, primary, or support).
3. Create a bullet list of the major outputs created by the process. The output can be in the form of a physical product, information product, completed task, or some other tangible or predictable result of the process action. It is the "what" of process, not the "why."
4. List the customers (external or internal) that receive the major outputs. They are the primary source of the requirements specifications for the process output.
5. Identify the trigger or event that initiates the process to start. The trigger is the input, event, or condition that sets the process in motion.
6. Create a bullet list of the inputs that are required by the process to convert them into outputs. Inputs are materials, information, or other resources that are required, in addition to the trigger, in order for the process to function correctly.
7. Identify the suppliers that provide inputs to the process. Suppliers can be internal or external, and may be expressed as either a process or an organization.
8. Use this information as an aid in developing your process relationship map.

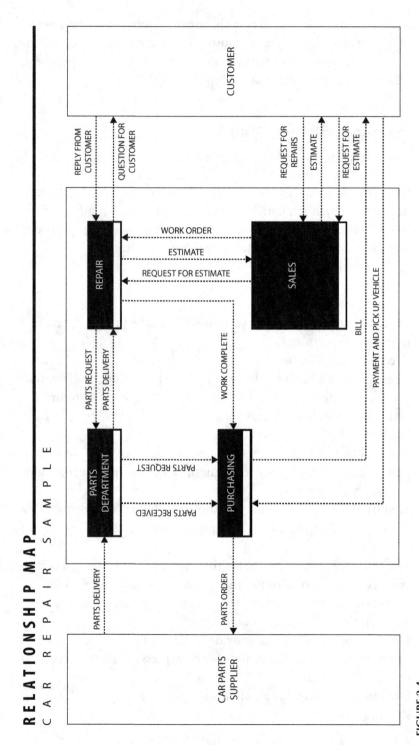

FIGURE 2.4
Sample relationship map.

How to Interpret a Relationship Map

Relationship maps show how the parts of an organization are wired together. They can help you better understand who does what to whom and what the customer and supplier links are throughout the organization. Relationship maps that are drawn correctly are easy to interpret. Arrows show the flow of goods, services, and ideas—the inputs and outputs. Suppliers and customers are easily depicted.

Why Use a Relationship Map?

Process relationship maps allow you to

- Depict the way an entire enterprise, business unit, or function operates
- Prioritize process improvement projects and operational investments
- Identify potential disconnects, failure points, or bottlenecks within the organization's business system
- Communicate the "essence" of the business to others
- Reveal logical locations to measure performance
- Compare one business model to another
- Compare the current state of the business processes to a future state
- Better understand what out-of-scope processes may have an impact on targeted processes

 A relationship map is a process and visual tool used to outline cause-and-effect relationships. The process of creating a relationship diagram helps a group analyze the natural links between different aspects of a complex situation, project or problem.

Flowchart

A flowchart is an easy-to-understand diagram that shows how the steps in a process fit together. The simplicity of flowcharts makes them useful tools for communicating how processes work, and for documenting how to do a particular job. Furthermore, the act of mapping out a process using a flowchart can clarify your understanding of it and help you improve it.

You can use them to

- Define and analyze processes
- Communicate steps to other people involved in a process
- Identify bottlenecks

- Standardize a process
- Improve a process
- Troubleshoot a problem

A flowchart uses shapes, words, and arrows to create a visual diagram of a specific process. Every step in the process becomes a shape on the diagram. Short text notes within each shape provide the details regarding the process. Flowcharts rely heavily on shape recognition and symbols to ensure information can be reviewed and ingested quickly—even when the process is fairly complex. Figure 2.5 illustrates a sample flowchart.

How to Create Flowcharts

The main steps to construct a flowchart are as follows:

1. Identify the process to be diagrammed.
2. Identify the start and end of the process you are describing or documenting.
3. Arrange all the required activities in proper order. Also, ensure that the dependencies between processes are clearly documented. You may not need to go into detail, but it should be noted at a high level.
4. Once the activities are documented and you have agreement that the sequence of activities is correct, use arrows to indicate the flow of the diagram.
5. Ensure agreement and alignment on the documented process.

How to Interpret Flowcharts

Flowcharts are generally easy to interpret, even to the untrained eye. A good flowchart should be intuitive so that the eye naturally begins with the start of the process. You usually read a flowchart from top to bottom or from left to right, and arrows should guide the reader through each step of the process. Simple shapes with text inside indicate actions, decisions, and the beginning and end of a process. Connectors in the form of arrows indicate relationships and the direction of the process. Ovals are used to show where a process begins and ends, for example, and diamonds indicate that a decision is being made, which causes the process to branch in one of two directions. A rectangle indicates a specific activity, and the input and output from activities are depicted through an arrow.

FLOWCHART
SAMPLE STORE CHECKOUT PROCESS

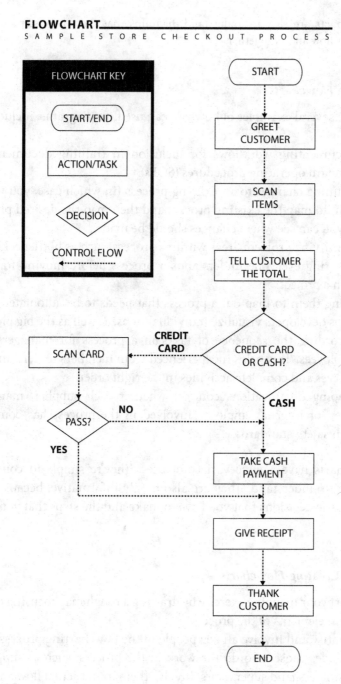

FIGURE 2.5
Sample flowchart.

Flowcharts are easy to understand diagrams that show how steps in a process flow and fit together.

Why Use Flowcharts?

There are several examples of how you can use flow diagrams, including

- Documenting workflows for inclusion in training documents or standard operating procedures (SOPs).
- Planning changes to an existing process (in which case, you would want to map the existing process and then map the desired process so you can see where changes should be made).
- Identifying problem areas within a process, such as bottlenecks.
- Ensuring everyone understands a process before moving forward with a project.
- Using them to map out a process that needs to be automated. This helps developers visualize individual steps, as well as the big picture.
- Recording the sequence of tasks in a process for managers and employees. This helps inexperienced team members understand the process and complete activities in the right order.
- Helping organizations confirm whether each supplier, manufacturer, or internal employee involved in the process has complied with safety standards.

Flowcharts have a wide variety of uses. They're simple to construct and easy to understand. They are also highly informative, because they illustrate the decisions that you have to make and the steps that you need to take.

Tips for Creating Flowcharts

- Start your mapping exercise by drawing a rough map focusing on the main elements of the process.
- Identify and involve all key people in the flowcharting process. This includes those who do the work in the process, such as suppliers, customers, and supervisors. Involve them in the actual flowcharting sessions or by interviewing them before the sessions, as well as by showing them the developing flowchart between work sessions and obtaining their feedback.

- Don't worry too much about drawing the flowchart the right way. The right way is the way that helps those involved understand the process.
- Computer software is available for drawing flowcharts.
- Do not assign a technical expert to draw the flowchart. A process analyst or one of the people who actually perform the process should do it.
- Although you can draw flowcharts by hand, it's often much more convenient to use process mapping tools. This makes flowcharts easier to amend, and they can then be stored in a format that can be retrieved easily.

Cross-Functional Map

A cross-functional diagram, sometimes called a swim lane map, is a process map that provides richer information than a traditional flowchart. It can be expanded to show who does what, when tasks are done, and how long they take. The diagram uses a lot of the same shapes and notations that you find on a flowchart, but it divides the entire process into functions, or swim lanes, which make it easy to see what areas or persons are responsible for each step in the workflow. They can help you elaborate on what is originally drawn in a simple flowchart. Figure 2.6 outlines a sample layout for a cross-functional map.

How to Create a Cross-Functional Map

The main steps to construct a cross-functional map are as follows:

1. Similar to the flowchart, ensure you've identified your start and end points. These should be well-defined triggers, outputs, or events.
2. It is then important to determine and document the lanes of your diagram. What are the departments, functions, or people you are dividing the flowchart by? You could also label the swim lanes with people or groups, such as report submitter, processor, approver, and check writer.
3. Add steps to your swim lane diagram in the same way you add them to a flowchart, except steps must be presented both in a logical order and under their respective function or group.
4. It is often recommended to trace activities back from the end of a process to the beginning to force true analytical thinking and drive out inaccuracy.

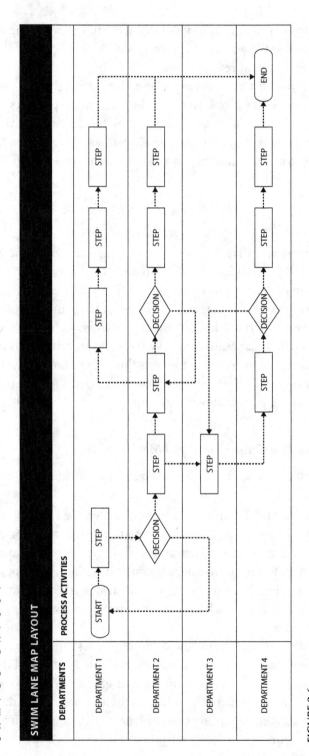

FIGURE 2.6
Sample cross-functional map.

Key Features

Although the cross-functional maps carry many of the same features or benefits as those of the flowcharts, a swim lane diagram differs because it has the added benefit of depicting handoffs between distinct entities. Ultimately, cross-functional maps have three key features:

1. *Swim lanes*: Horizontal bands that show work activities in the context of each department responsible for executing a process
2. *Workflow*: Interrelated activities and resources deployed to execute a process
3. *Supplier–customer relationships*: The interface among internal organizations and external customers and suppliers of the organization

How to Interpret a Cross-Functional Map

Interpreting a cross-functional map is done similarly to a flowchart—the symbols and shapes mean the same thing. Swim lanes provide you with added information at a glance, by describing which functional area each of the activities occurs in.

There are several common mapping conventions that improve the legibility of a cross-functional process map. These include

- Using boxes to show the steps that make up the process.
- Drawing lines with arrowheads to show an input or an output associated with each step. If possible, label any inputs and outputs so that when you analyze the process, you can see the transformation or value of each step.
- As best as possible, trying to keep the flow or sequence of steps moving from left to right.
- Avoiding confusing intersections of flow lines by using over and under lines.
- Using a diamond-shaped box to indicate when a decision is made in the process. Be sure to label the decision and the decision outcomes from the diamond.
- Drawing horizontal bands, also known as swim lanes, to represent the different functional areas that participate in the process. Be sure to label each band. Put the end customer of the process in the topmost band.

- If several areas jointly perform the same step, drawing the step box so that it includes (i.e., crosses over) all the areas involved.

Why Use a Cross-Functional Map?

You would create a cross-functional map for all the same reasons you would create a basic flowchart. Instances where you might choose the cross-functional map over a basic flowchart include

- When mapping processes that extend across multiple departments or functions
- When mapping a complex process and swim lanes help you break it down visually
- When categorizing areas of the process might help you attach labor hours or expenses to certain departments or cost centers

Tips for Creating Cross-Functional Maps

- When defining departments for swim lanes, don't necessarily take the term *department* literally. In many cases, swim lanes could represent a single person, part of a department, a physical entity, or a different company altogether.
- When disagreements arise on mapping activities, take the necessary time to resolve them so that the final model truly reflects common understanding.
- Always remember that disagreements often represent good opportunities for clarifying potential conflicts of misunderstanding.
- If you use a classical paper, marker, and Post-it method for mapping out your process, always remember to transpose it into written form or draw it in a professional software tool so the work is not lost.

Value Stream Map

Value stream mapping is a process improvement tool that outlines activities in high detail for every step of a process. Many Lean practitioners see value stream mapping as a fundamental tool to identify waste, reduce process cycle times, and implement process improvement. Some organizations treat the practice of value stream mapping as a hallmark of their process improvement efforts. Although frequently associated with manufacturing environments, the tenants of value stream mapping can be used to map a variety of processes in all industries, including healthcare, software development, service, supply chain, logistics, and product development. Figure 2.7 outlines a sample value stream map.

How to Create a Value Stream Map

There is not one way to create a value stream map, but the most common steps are as follows:

- Identify the target product or service.
- Gather a team of experts and people with strong knowledge of the process.
- Identify the actions that take place in order to create that product or service.
- Author a value stream map that depicts the process steps, information flows, and timelines that are required to create the product or service being analyzed. The mapping can be either a design, production, or service flow and may use standardized value mapping process symbols.
- Specify the calendar time over which these actions are worked on.
- Specify how much time was spent waiting between each step, and how much time is spent on each activity.
- Look for and denote any loop-backs present in the workflow.
- Develop a list of opportunities for improvement based on these observations.
- Redraw the mapping as a future state value stream map with the wasteful steps removed.
- Implement process changes in the organization to work toward the new value stream mapping.

Key Features

A value stream map is an excellent tool to use to communicate to your stakeholders what is not functioning today and your suggestions for improvement. It may take several iterations before you reach your ideal state; however, documenting your value stream map based on your current state and highlighting your suggested improvements is a great start. Key features of value stream maps include

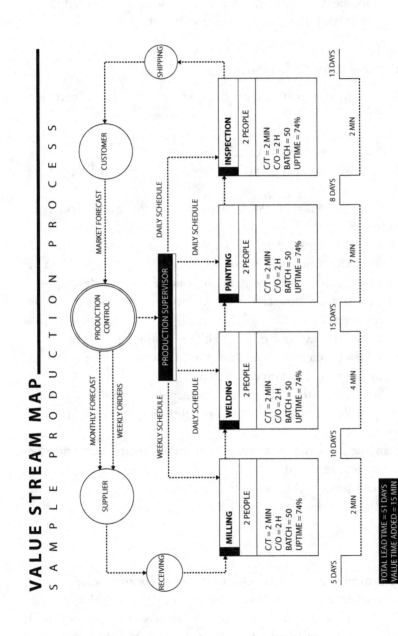

FIGURE 2.7
Sample value stream map.

- Activities and connectors
- Inputs and outputs from each step over a time period, such as a minute, hour, day, or work shift
- Average amount of inventory held at each step in the process
- Cycle time (total time required to produce a product or service)
- Number of operators
- Uptime of machinery, equipment, and systems
- Downtime of machinery, equipment, and systems
- Number of hours worked per activity
- Total work time
- Batch size or volumes
- Any waste

How to Interpret a Value Stream Map

When the technique is used, the process's value-added steps are depicted horizontally across the center of the map. Vertical lines that are at right angles to the value stream depict non-value-added steps. The vertical line indicates the steps for creating the product or service at that particular stage of the overall process, with the overall goal being to create a new mapping that has minimum delay.

Why Use a Value Stream Map?

- It helps you visualize more than just the single-process level, for example, assembly or welding.
- It provides a common language for talking about processes.
- It helps you see the sources of waste in your process.
- It ties together process improvement concepts and techniques.
- It makes decisions about the flow apparent, so you can discuss it openly. Otherwise, many details and decisions on your shop floor just happen by default or even by chance.
- It shows the linkage between the information flow and the material flow.
- It forms the basis of an implementation plan. By helping you design how the whole door-to-door flow should operate, the map becomes a blueprint for process improvement.
- It is useful as both a quantitative and diagramming tool, as it produces a tally of non-value-added steps, lead time, distance traveled,

the amount of inventory, and so on. Displaying numbers and counts right on the map is often beneficial for creating a sense of urgency or before and after measures.

Tips for Creating Value Stream Maps

- When possible, always collect current state information by observing.
- Ask as many performance-related questions as possible as you walk through the process with stakeholders.
- Try to begin at the end of the process and work backwards.

WHAT DO PROCESS MAPS CONSIST OF?

The information included on a process map often depends on the type of process map you create; the purpose of the map; the scope, scale, and objectives of the process improvement project; and the information available to the team. Common parts of various process maps are defined below (Figure 2.8):

- *Participants*: The people, groups, units, or departments that are involved in executing the process, usually defined as anyone who touches the process from the starting point to the finishing point.
- *Process owner*: The individual responsible for the day-to-day operation of the process—usually a supervisor, department head, or executive leader.
- *Sponsor*: A high-level individual with the ability to directly provide resources for a process or influence provision of resources, such as labor or capital.
- *Suppliers*: Individuals, groups, vendors, or departments that provide inputs to a project—might include both in-house or outside entities.
- *Cycle times*: The time it takes for one item to make it from the beginning to the end of a process or step.
- *Systems*: Nonperson components of a process, including machines, automations, and computers.
- *Inputs*: Goods, ideas, or work items that enter the process in some raw form.

PROCESS MAP COMPONENTS
C O M M O N   F E A T U R E S

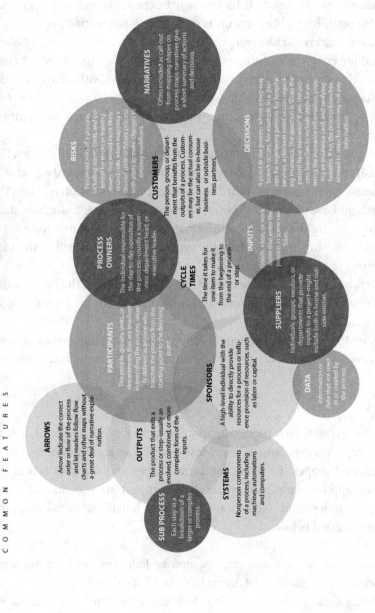

NARRATIVES

Often included as call-out from mapping shapes on process maps, narratives give a short summary of actions and decisions.

RISKS

Perceived risks of a process, including waste, costs, and potential for errors or training issues. You would most likely record risks when mapping a desired state of future process with plans to make changes to existing workflows.

CUSTOMERS

The person, group, or department that benefits from the outputs of a process. Customers may be the actual consumer, but can also be in-house business or outside business partners.

DECISIONS

A point in the process where a two-way branch occurs, for example in a process for registering patients for hospital services, a decision point occurs regarding insurance. The question is "Does the patient have insurance." If yes, the process branches to include steps for entering the insurance information, copying an insurance card, and verifying benefits. If no, the process branches instead to steps for entering self-pay information.

PROCESS OWNERS

The individual responsible for the day-to-day operation of the process—usually a supervisor, department head, or executive leader.

CYCLE TIMES

The time it takes for one item to make it from the beginning to the end of a process or step.

INPUTS

Goods, ideas, or work items that enter the process in some raw form.

PARTICIPANTS

The people, groups, units, or departments that are involved in executing the process, usually defined as anyone who touches the process from the starting point to the finishing point

SPONSORS

A high-level individual with the ability to directly provide resources for a process or influence provision of resources, such as labor or capital.

SUPPLIERS

Individuals, groups, vendors, or departments that provide inputs to a project—might include both in-house and outside entities.

ARROWS

Arrow indicate the correct order or flow of the process and let readers follow flow charts and other maps without a great deal of narrative explanation.

OUTPUTS

The product that exits a process or step—usually an evolved, combined, or more complete form of the inputs.

DATA

Information or data that are used in or created by the process.

SYSTEMS

Nonperson components of a process, including machines, automations and computers.

SUB PROCESS

Each step in a breakdown of a larger or complex process.

FIGURE 2.8

Common process mapping features and components.

- *Outputs*: The product that exits a process or step—usually an evolved, combined, or more complete form of the inputs.
- *Data*: Information or data that are used in or created by the process.
- *Customers*: The person, group, or department that benefits from the outputs of a process. Customers may be the actual consumer, but can also be in-house business units or outside business partners.
- *Risks*: Perceived risks of a process, including waste, costs, and potential for errors or training issues. You would most likely record risks when mapping a desired state or future process with plans to make changes to existing workflows.
- *Subprocesses*: Each step in a breakdown of a larger or complex process.
- *Decisions*: A point in the process where a two-way branch occurs. For example, in a process for registering patients for hospital services, a decision point occurs regarding insurance. The question is "Does the patient have insurance?" If yes, the process branches to include steps for entering the insurance information, copying an insurance card, and verifying benefits. If no, the process branches instead to steps for entering self-pay information.
- *Arrows*: Arrows indicate the correct order or flow of the process and let readers follow flowcharts and other maps without a great deal of narrative explanation.
- *Narratives*: Often included as callout from mapping shapes on process maps, narratives give a short summary of actions and decisions.

Shapes

As you've learned, each process map uses various symbols and shapes to denote steps, actions, and items. Most people use a common system of notation and shapes. By using the same shapes and symbols across the process mapping world, you create diagrams that are easy for all stakeholders to understand. Common shapes and notations across mapping types are defined below.

- *Start* and *end symbols*, represented as lozenges, ovals or rounded rectangles, usually containing the word "Start" or "End".
- *Arrows*, showing what's called "flow of control" or "flow of process". An arrow coming from one symbol and ending at another symbol signifies flow passes to the symbol the arrow points to.

- *Processing steps*, represented as rectangles. Examples include "Submit approval"; "replace identified part"; "save changes", or similar.
- *Input/Output*, represented as a parallelogram. Examples: Get "X" from the user; display "X".
- *Decision*, represented as a diamond (rhombus). These typically contain a "Yes/No" question or "True/False" test. This symbol is unique in that it has two arrows coming out of it, usually from the bottom point and right point, one corresponding to "Yes" or "True", and one corresponding to "No" or "False". The arrows should always be labeled. More than two arrows can be used, but this is normally a clear indicator that a complex decision is being taken, in which case it may need to be broken-down further, or replaced with the "pre-defined or sub-process" symbol.'
- A number of other symbols that have less universal currency, such as
  - A *document* represented as a rectangle with a wavy base.
  - A *manual input* represented by a rectangle, with the top irregularly sloping up from left to right. An example would be to signify data-entry from a form.
  - A *manual operation* represented by a trapezoid with the longest parallel side uppermost, to represent an operation or adjustment to process that can only be made manually.
  - A *data file* represented by a cylinder.
  - *Connectors*, usually represented as circles, to represent converging paths in a flowchart.

 There are many other symbols, in addition to those highlighted above. However, remember that flowcharts are used for communication. If you use symbols that only a few people understand, there's a good chance that your message will fail. As always, keep things simple.

WHAT ARE THE STAGES OF PROCESS MAPPING?

Although each mapping type has detailed steps that are unique, all mapping exercises ultimately follow a common pattern or set of steps. This section provides a high-level overview of the common steps involved in a business process mapping exercise. To create a process map, you need to identify the key process objectives and main activity steps. When collecting and analyzing information about the process, you should consider such factors as process complexity, the number of organizational and individual teams involved, and time and cost issues. The process map should highlight bottlenecks and delays, required rework times, unnecessary work steps, and any ambiguities within a process. It is recommended that you represent the process flow from the customer's point of view, thus showing whether each step of the process helps create a clear value for the customer. The following four steps will help guide you through the planning and execution of any process mapping activity:

1. Plan the mapping effort.
2. Form and train the mapping team.
3. Conduct the mapping session.
4. Review and revise the process map.

Plan the Mapping Effort

- The first step is to clearly define the process to be mapped and designate the boundaries of the process. What are the triggers that begin the process? What are the outputs or consequences that end the process? Is this tied to a specific project or is mapping a project of its own?
- If the mapping project is tied to a specific project, consider using the same sponsor as that project, or determine a new sponsor for the effort.
- The next step is to determine the organizational departments to be included in the process map. Is this a process that cuts across business units, or is it confined to a single business unit? Does the process involve several functions or just one? How many work groups are involved?
- Another important and difficult step is to determine the level of detail that will be included in the process map. Will only key process steps be included, or will specific tasks within steps also be portrayed? Will individual assignments be noted or just overall work group responsibilities?
- The process elements to be described in the map must also be defined. Process inputs, outputs, action steps, and performers should be included in all process maps. Optional elements include the time

required to complete each step, feedback to the performer, systems, data elements, business rules, work environment, and other attributes of the process.

- The media and format used to create the process map also require planning. Will a computer software program or a manual process mapping be employed? Will a third-party facilitator be used?
- Also important is ensuring success is planning the logistics of the process mapping session, such as meeting rooms, food, mapping materials such as paper, markers, and adhesive notes if needed, and computers.

Form and Train the Process Mapping Team

- Select the people who will form the process mapping team. The team should include the process owner, the individual with overall responsibility for the routine management of the process, and the employees who play key roles in the process. If many employees participate in the process, it will be necessary to select a representative from each work group. It is usually best to limit the team to 8 to 10 people to keep the process workshop manageable.
- Before the actual process mapping session, schedule a training session to review the basic concepts and methods of process mapping. As the team learns, it is best to practice with a familiar process, such as planning a vacation or hosting a festive party. This type of mapping practice can be very effective in preparing the team to efficiently map the target process.

Conduct the Mapping Session

- When the team assembles, begin with a quick review of the mapping process, and then reach consensus on the departments or other entities involved in the process.
- Lead the team through identifying each step in the process. As each step is identified, write it in the row of the group that performs that step.
- When all process steps have been agreed on and placed on the map, walk through the map step-by-step and discuss any changes or additions that need to be made. Rearrange, add, or discard activities as needed.

- Review the revised map again with the team and make any further changes or additions.
- Number the steps by placing sequential numbers in activity.
- Before the team adjourns, review all acronyms, abbreviations, or special terms written on the notes to ensure they are understood by all and consistently used or documented for reference.
- Immediately after the mapping session, the facilitator should transfer the information on the paper map into a proper program to create an electronic version of the map if it was not done so directly in the event.

Review and Revise the Process Map

- Distribute copies of the map to the team for individual review. Meet briefly to confirm that the process was accurately captured and note any changes that need to be made.
- Make any changes needed, and then distribute the revised map to a larger group for review. This is an opportunity to solicit input from many people who participate or interact with the process.
- Use the feedback received to revise the process map as needed. It is now ready for use and can be circulated and published.

CLOSING REMARKS

The aim of process mapping is to make things clear and provide insight. The best map is often the simplest map. There are different approaches to mapping processes, procedures, and work instructions and which one you select will depend on

- What you need to know
- Resources and timescales
- What level you are working at
- Engagement and interest of staff

Each one gives you a slightly different perspective, and there is no definitive right or wrong. When you first start process mapping, it is not unusual to find that processes include steps that serve no discernable purpose at all. These steps are remnants from earlier processes or projects that may no longer be necessary. It is also possible that you will uncover duplicate activities done by multiple people or teams, or that there is disagreement as to which person or department actually performs activities, or even whether the activity is actually performed at all. Process mapping provides clarity by ensuring that everybody understands the process and helps eliminate duplication, overlap, and omission of key steps. Quickly eliminating wastes and redundancies makes it easy for the organization to see the value in process mapping, and mapping out processes lets teams design new workflows with better outcomes, find issues with existing processes, and document procedures for training or audit purposes.

Although simple in concept, process mapping can be complex and must be carefully planned. You must work out how exactly you are going to perform the exercise, determine the right mapping type and technique, and allocate the necessary resources and appropriate staff to the mapping exercise. The end result should be a set of useful process flows and a process landscape for the enterprise to rally behind.

3

Managing Process Improvements

Think of a successful organization, regardless of industry. One of the measures of its ultimate success is its agility, whether it manages to stay at least one step ahead of its market or competitors. Achieving real alignment, where strategy, goals, and process improvement reinforce one another, gives an organization a major advantage because it has a clearer sense of what to do at any given time, and employees are able to constantly move in the right direction. The result is an organization that can focus less on deciding what to do and more on simply doing, improving, and evolving.

When people understand and are excited about the direction their company is taking, they ultimately become more engaged and motivated. High-achieving organizations are also better than others at turning their visions into viable strategies that guide operational planning and improvement, something many business leaders may believe they already do well, but which often proves difficult in practice. Even more prevalent is the breakdown in vision at the individual or project level, where employees see only the gap between leadership goals and their daily work lives.

Some organizations, though, are able to manage these links effectively, whereby vision, strategy, and goals come together to drive meaningful process improvement efforts. These organizations typically have a basic framework in place to help drive organizational planning and process improvement initiatives. The main reason for developing an agreed upon framework is that it provides structure for setting process improvement priorities, creating project standards, resolving conflict and disputes, and outlining the fundamental principles that guide process improvement within an organization. By having a framework in place, companies instill a sense of empowerment and achievement that, in turn, enables their people to continually achieve more and more. This chapter outlines a basic framework for driving process improvement and transformation within any company.

By the end of this chapter, you should be able to

- Describe the importance of strategy and process improvement
- Explain the characteristics of a process improvement framework
- List the benefits of a process improvement framework
- Outline the roles involved in process improvement efforts
- Identify the five phases needed to improve business processes

WHAT IS A PROCESS IMPROVEMENT FRAMEWORK?

Governance over process improvement efforts is often discussed, but rarely explained in the context of a framework that can be applied to a variety of enterprise types. It is traditionally thought of as the way in which enterprises are directed and controlled, but more recently, it has been defined as the framework of phases and procedures by which decisions in an enterprise are made, projects are executed, and responsible parties are held accountable for outcomes. A process improvement framework therefore provides a standard outline for driving strategy and building and improving processes quickly and collaboratively, while ensuring high performance across a company. It is a set of standards, methods, policies, and constraints used to help employees in different roles identify, measure, and improve the performance of the business processes that make up their company.

As organizations improve and standardize their systems and business processes to maximize productivity, they should also follow a structured approach that will lead to consistent, predictable, and reliable solution design and performance improvement. Deploying a common process improvement framework offers a consistent life cycle to stakeholders as process improvement projects are executed. Organizations that deploy a management framework that governs all of their transformation projects help ensure accountability and responsibility for any changes that are made during process improvements. Whether the work is done departmentally, cross-functionally, or through a centralized process improvement team, common language, methods, tools, architectures, and metrics are needed to ensure that multidisciplinary teams of professionals across an enterprise can work together efficiently. In this way, companies can harness the power of a common management framework to achieve consistently high performance and process improvement results.

 Framework is a structure intended to serve as a support or guide for the building, improvement, or delivery of something that expands operations or delivers something useful or of value to an organization.

Several benefits of developing a process improvement framework include

- Ensuring strategic planning and communication occur
- Providing a common approach to building business cases and proposing improvements
- Focusing attention on the most important improvements and their benefits
- Improving communications with stakeholders by providing measures for planned changes
- Improving the chances of successful business change by focusing on final outcomes
- Identifying, managing, and mitigating the risks associated with process improvements and the realization of their benefits
- Increasing quality and productivity through improvement initiatives
- Creating flexibility in solution management
- Improving teamwork
- Cultivating an enterprise-wide outlook among teams
- Increasing customer satisfaction by improving the quality and speed of outputs
- Ensuring proper accountability is in place for improvements
- Providing a mechanism for independent review or audit

Although many process improvement methodologies have been developed over the years, most of them go through a common set of phases. The process improvement framework outlined in this chapter aims to provide a simple framework that would help any organization think about,

PROCESS IMPROVEMENT FRAMEWORK _____
PHASES OF PROCESS IMPROVEMENT

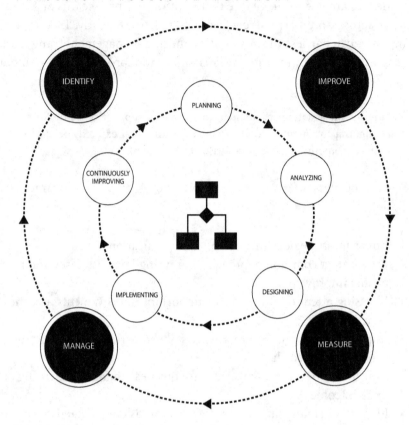

FIGURE 3.1
Phases of process improvement.

describe, and improve its business processes in a logical, strategic, and self-reflective manner. Figure 3.1 depicts the major pillars and phases of the process improvement framework.

HOW DO PROCESS IMPROVEMENT AND STRATEGY ALIGN?

Organizations that are starting their process improvement journey typically find themselves in one of two groupings when it comes to their visions. The first group consists of companies whose visions have weakened, which often occurs out of neglect or inconsistent understanding across the organization. An organization whose vision focuses on quality and operational efficiency may discover that the decisions it made to increase efficiency have undermined quality. Or the organization that seeks to drive results finds that internal competition among organizations has reduced organizational focus, leading to declines in almost every area.

The second group consists of organizations whose visions are still quite strong, but where changing circumstances, such as technological developments, economic conditions, or perhaps new market openings, mean that they will no longer be able to achieve their vision in the same way and thus process transformation is needed. Organizations in the first category must start by realigning according to what the vision should be. Organizations in the second category may omit this step, but may face even larger challenges later on, when convincing their people that despite today's success, the strategy and goals that implement the vision must change radically in light of external conditions.

Building a Vision for the Future

The first step toward strategic harmony is building a vision for the future. What sort of values do you wish to promote in your organization? What sort of markets do you hope to conquer? Who are your ultimate customers? What strategic opportunities are you targeting and why? What disruptors or threats do you hope to avert? A truly sound vision is only effective if it balances multiple dimensions at once. First, it must be broad enough to be recognized by everybody, even in a large and diversified company, yet it must also be adequately specific to differentiate the organization clearly from its competitors. It must be enduring enough to serve the organization over the long term, while also allowing its execution to change as the enterprise evolves. It must articulate ideals while describing how the organization wants to progress in ways that seem achievable. And, to be truly compelling, it must outline how the changes will affect the employees themselves, their departments, their customers, the organization as a whole, and any markets.

Within those guidelines, there is no particular vision that appears to offer a distinct advantage; for example, organizations have been equally successful with visions focused on growth, market share, cost, sales, or even external constraints. What matters is that the organization finds the right vision for itself and then communicates and pursues it in a way that is relevant, timely, concrete, and meaningful.

Creating a Strategy

To be successful means knowing how to use your talent and resources to the best of your ability. It is very difficult to execute your organizational vision if you don't have a proper strategic plan in place. A vision is of little value on its own unless it becomes a part of your company strategy and supports a tangible set of organizational goals. Together, they outline where the organization's competitive advantage will come from and how it will be sustained.

To determine your strategy, you must fully understand the internal and external environmental factors that affect you. With that understanding, you can identify your clear advantages and use these to make informed choices and implement your strategy effectively. In doing so, you ensure that the right processes and areas are selected for transformation and that they have the right level of attention to ensure sustained improvement.

Strategy creation follows a simple three-stage process:

- Analyzing the context in which you're operating and assess against your vision for the future
- Identifying strategic options
- Evaluating and selecting the best processes and process areas for transformation, change, or improvement

With your strategy in place, you now must choose the best strategic improvements or improvement areas, making sure that you don't choose too many options and spread your resources too thinly. Your strategy tells you how you'll achieve success, no matter how that success is defined. And whether you're developing a strategy at the team or organizational level, the planning process is as important as the outcome. Identify your unique capabilities, and understand how to use these to your advantage while minimizing threats.

Communicating Change and Setting Targets

Connecting your vision and strategy to people's daily work is the last step in achieving strategic alignment across your company, and how you communicate that strategy and improvement vision can be challenging. If you communicate the outline too early, before people can see any evidence that change is needed, the organization risks losing credibility and people may view the transformation as yet another corporate initiative destined to fail. Conversely, if the organization communicates the changes too late, particularly if the changes will have an effect on the workforce, like reductions, rumors may begin to spread, causing even greater damage to transformation efforts and, more importantly, morale.

In our experience, beginning with areas where quick wins and improvement can be made and using those early successes to help refine the organization's strategy is most successful. As these wins begin to spread throughout the organization, managers and their people adapt the vision to their group's work, giving the vision the ground-up credibility needed to ensure sustainability. These groups and employees become stewards of process improvement, helping create new goals that reinforce the process improvement vision.

As people at all levels begin to understand the need for process improvement, they also begin to see the effects of the various process improvements. Ultimately, it is this visibility that has the greatest impact on employees and will help promote problem solving and continuous improvement.

Overall, here are some key questions to consider as you build a vision and strategic outlook for your company:

- What are your organizational strengths, weaknesses, opportunities, and threats, and what are your core competencies?
- What other environmental factors may affect organizational progress?
- What is your organization capable of achieving if you focus resources accordingly?
- What are the big-picture trends in your market?
- How can you monitor or adapt to these external factors?
- Who are the stakeholders who are important to your success (suppliers, customers, etc.)?
- What options do you have?
- Which of these should you consider?

Check your proposed project or process improvement ideas for consistency with your organization's vision, mission, and values and update these if necessary as new problems and improvement opportunities are brought forward. It's easy to forget about these critical elements during strategic planning, so ensure that what you want to do is something that contributes toward the organization's overall purpose and truly solves problems or contributes value.

WHAT ARE THE PHASES OF PROCESS IMPROVEMENT?

Most process improvement frameworks, although driven by strategy, are supported by five phases that are equally important and necessary. This section guides you through each phase and provides an overview of each for you to use along your improvement journey. These phases can be used to execute process improvement initiatives.

The five major stages that are common in most process improvement frameworks are

1. **Plan** the process improvement effort. This includes defining the vision, objectives, and potential benefits, ensuring alignment with strategic drivers.
   - Has a problem been identified and defined appropriately?
   - Have the high-level benefits been identified and estimated?
   - Have the vision, objectives, and end state been articulated?
   - Have the key stakeholders been identified?
   - Has an improvement realization strategy been developed?
2. **Analyze** the process or processes targeted for transformation or causing pain points.
   - Has the baseline set of processes to analyze been agreed with key stakeholders?
   - Have process owners been consulted and confirmed?
   - Have current state process maps and profiles been developed and verified?
   - Has a disconnect or pain point register been established?
3. **Design** the process improvements by identifying and presenting recommendations on specific trouble areas and designing a road map to support improvement implementation.
   - Have future state process maps and profiles been developed and endorsed?
   - Have implications of potential process designs and changes been considered?
   - Have proposed improvements been tested?
   - Have all necessary stakeholders been included in process design efforts?
   - Does the proposed design solve the root cause of problems and pain points identified?

- Have implementation obstacles been considered?
4. Effectively manage the improvement **implementation** and subsequent process operations using a clearly defined, approved approach.
    - Have all necessary parties been communicated with?
    - Have stakeholders been educated and familiarized with changes and improvements?
    - Has a pilot of the newly designed process or processes been conducted?
    - Have previous artifacts, reference materials, and guides been removed and replaced with new collateral?
    - Have technology changes been deployed and verified?
    - Has the new process been formally rolled out?
5. In order to maintain process health and recognize ongoing improvement opportunities, it is essential to continuously measure performance and **continuously improve** key elements.
    - Have process monitoring and reporting been established?
    - Have quick wins been realized?
    - Has progress been reviewed against the business case?
    - Has the disconnect register been reviewed and updated?
    - Has the transition to operations been managed?
    - Has progress toward the vision or end state been reported?
    - Have lessons learned been captured and communicated?

 Not all stages may be relevant to your program or project, but you can use this standard approach to focus on developing your own improvements.

Figure 3.2 provides a pictorial representation of the phases of process improvement from strategy through continuous improvement.

Planning

The key to applying the framework is to understand your starting point. One of the first steps in any process improvement journey is defining what it is you'll be working on. What needs fixing, what is the expected outcome, and what is the scope within which the team will work? In order to effectively plan a process improvement project, you must determine if an improvement is even needed. Many telling signs exist that help you answer that question, including

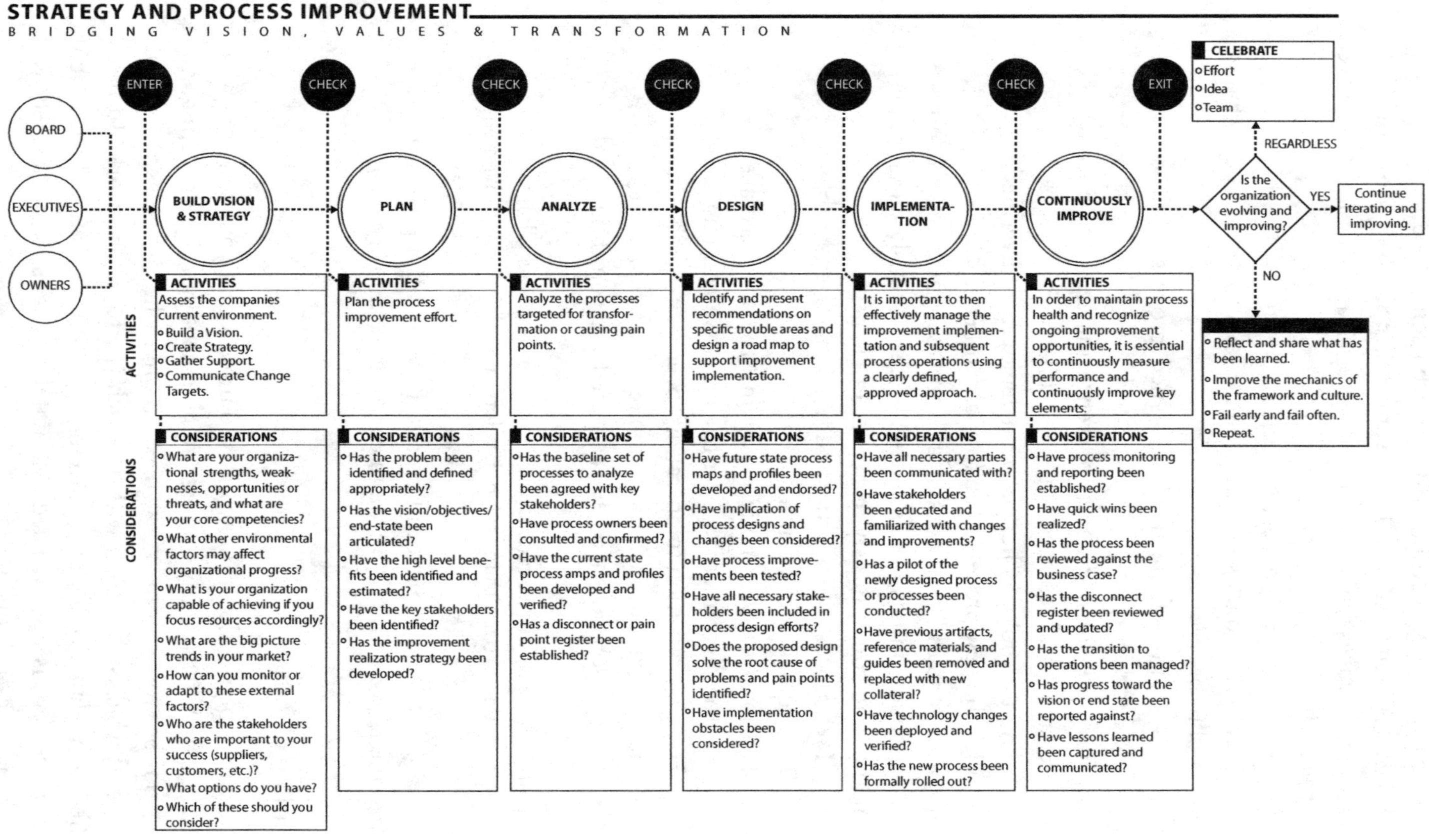

STRATEGY AND PROCESS IMPROVEMENT
BRIDGING VISION, VALUES & TRANSFORMATION

BOARD
EXECUTIVES
OWNERS

ENTER

CHECK / CHECK / CHECK / CHECK / CHECK / CHECK

BUILD VISION & STRATEGY

PLAN

ANALYZE

DESIGN

IMPLEMENTA-TION

CONTINUOUSLY IMPROVE

EXIT

CELEBRATE
- Effort
- Idea
- Team

REGARDLESS

Is the organization evolving and improving?

YES — Continue iterating and improving.

NO

- Reflect and share what has been learned.
- Improve the mechanics of the framework and culture.
- Fail early and fail often.
- Repeat.

ACTIVITIES

BUILD VISION & STRATEGY — ACTIVITIES
Assess the companies current environment.
- Build a Vision.
- Create Strategy.
- Gather Support.
- Communicate Change Targets.

PLAN — ACTIVITIES
Plan the process improvement effort.

ANALYZE — ACTIVITIES
Analyze the processes targeted for transformation or causing pain points.

DESIGN — ACTIVITIES
Identify and present recommendations on specific trouble areas and design a road map to support improvement implementation.

IMPLEMENTATION — ACTIVITIES
It is important to then effectively manage the improvement implementation and subsequent process operations using a clearly defined, approved approach.

CONTINUOUSLY IMPROVE — ACTIVITIES
In order to maintain process health and recognize ongoing improvement opportunities, it is essential to continuously measure performance and continuously improve key elements.

CONSIDERATIONS

BUILD VISION & STRATEGY — CONSIDERATIONS
- What are your organizational strengths, weaknesses, opportunities or threats, and what are your core competencies?
- What other environmental factors may affect organizational progress?
- What is your organization capable of achieving if you focus resources accordingly?
- What are the big picture trends in your market?
- How can you monitor or adapt to these external factors?
- Who are the stakeholders who are important to your success (suppliers, customers, etc.)?
- What options do you have? Which of these should you consider?

PLAN — CONSIDERATIONS
- Has the problem been identified and defined appropriately?
- Has the vision/objectives/end-state been articulated?
- Have the high level benefits been identified and estimated?
- Have the key stakeholders been identified?
- Has the improvement realization strategy been developed?

ANALYZE — CONSIDERATIONS
- Has the baseline set of processes to analyze been agreed with key stakeholders?
- Have process owners been consulted and confirmed?
- Have the current state process amps and profiles been developed and verified?
- Has a disconnect or pain point register been established?

DESIGN — CONSIDERATIONS
- Have future state process maps and profiles been developed and endorsed?
- Have implication of process designs and changes been considered?
- Have process improvements been tested?
- Have all necessary stakeholders been included in process design efforts?
- Does the proposed design solve the root cause of problems and pain points identified?
- Have implementation obstacles been considered?

IMPLEMENTATION — CONSIDERATIONS
- Have all necessary parties been communicated with?
- Have stakeholders been educated and familiarized with changes and improvements?
- Has a pilot of the newly designed process or processes been conducted?
- Have previous artifacts, reference materials, and guides been removed and replaced with new collateral?
- Have technology changes been deployed and verified?
- Has the new process been formally rolled out?

CONTINUOUSLY IMPROVE — CONSIDERATIONS
- Have process monitoring and reporting been established?
- Have quick wins been realized?
- Has the process been reviewed against the business case?
- Has the disconnect register been reviewed and updated?
- Has the transition to operations been managed?
- Has progress toward the vision or end state been reported against?
- Have lessons learned been captured and communicated?

FIGURE 3.2
Bridging strategy and process improvement.

- Coworkers or employees frequently expressing frustration about rework, bottlenecks, or errors
- Work being seemingly overcomplicated
- Customer feedback that product or service quality is subpar
- Things consistently taking longer and longer to complete
- Project and performance metrics continuing to underdeliver

Describe the Problem

Once a problem is identified, you need to define it, which is not always as easy as it sounds. Most people have a general understanding of the problem; they know something isn't working because goals aren't being met, for instance. But, a process improvement project must begin with a specific one- or two-sentence statement of the problem that includes answers to the five major question areas: who, what, when, where, and how. Specifically,

- Who does the problem affect?
- What is the service or product related to the problem?
- Where is the problem?
- When did the problem occur or when was it recorded?
- How big is the problem?

Identify the Scope of the Improvement

Once you know what you're working toward, you have to identify where the work needs to be done. Scope defines what will and won't be included in the project and how the initiative supports your organizational goals. What are the processes that need to be improved to reach the goal or solve the problem? What is the scale at which the project must operate? It is critical to clearly define the reach and impact of the process improvement in question. Understanding all process stakeholders and customers and where analysis focus must be directed drives the entire process improvement effort. Many managers see several symptoms of problematic processes occurring simultaneously, and that indicates that more than one process likely needs improvement. The planning phase identifies the start and end points of the effort and which processes must be analyzed. Prioritizing pain points and associated processes for analysis is key when looking to dive into complicated problems.

Create Project Charter

The problem, vision, and scope make up the foundation of a project charter, which is a short document that lets the team know what the project is about and who will be involved. The charter can also be presented to leadership to provide high-level, key information about the project, which is often required when presenting an initial project for approval to a sponsor or champion. It helps clarify how the problems or proposed improvements relate to other processes and stakeholders and creates a summary of how success will be measured, a list of all team members and their roles, and a list of key external and internal customers. The charter should also identify project leaders, including the project manager and process owner, and provide a target timeline for large milestones and total project completion. The project charter document ultimately contains standard, key elements found in the scoping of a process improvement initiative. These include

- Problem statement: background, objectives, scope, impacts, dependencies, assumptions and constraints, budget information
- High-level requirements
- High-level deliverables
- Timeline
- Level of effort
- Proposed team
- Stakeholder list

Conduct Readiness Assessment

A process improvement initiative must be adequately backed and endorsed by stakeholders who bring sufficient cooperation, energy, and resources to the effort. A readiness assessment is completed concurrently with the project charter using one-on-one interviews with stakeholders who have identified issues with the process in question. It is usually an internal, informal assessment, as opposed to the more formal project chartering exercise. At any time during the planning phase, the readiness assessment can be conducted and the determination whether to proceed with the improvement can be made. In many organizations, significant time and effort are put into formal charter and project development only to have it declined. Conducting readiness assessments proactively ensures little wasted effort.

Develop Roles and Responsibilities

Developing roles and responsibilities for process improvement projects is often difficult. It commonly begins with the question of ownership and responsibility as an organization begins to understand the value of processes and implement actions to manage those processes.

One of the most important questions to consider when embarking on a process journey is who should be selected as a process owner. But why is this difficult? Ironically, one of the most neglected areas of process improvement in any type of transformation is definition and assignment of roles and responsibilities. Although there is now a general acknowledgment that people are one of the, if not most critical, success factors in any type of business transformation, most organizations are not very accomplished at implementing people-oriented changes. In an attempt to understand this aspect of business process improvement, you need to define the responsibilities of an effective process owner. Assignment of process ownership is one of the indicators of an increasing level of process maturity.

The process owner is just one person required for a successful process improvement initiative, regardless of which methodology you decide to work within. One of the core principles of most improvement projects is that a multidisciplinary team, with representation from more than one department, is involved. The creation of the project team is where the foundation of a successful project is laid and roles and responsibilities are outlined (Figure 3.3). The makeup of the team is a reflection of the process to be improved. Some key roles on any process improvement project include

- *Sponsor or champion*: A person in leadership, usually at the executive level, that can champion a project when it comes to monetary, staffing, or other resource needs. Sometimes the sponsor commissions the project; other times, the team makes an initial presentation with a charter to seek approval and support from a sponsor. The sponsor is usually a member at either the steering or executive committee level within an organization.
- *Process owner*: Generally, the person responsible for the daily operation of the process or area that the improvement project will address. The business owner may be the one who suggested the project or may have been tapped by the sponsor to be a part of the project. In some

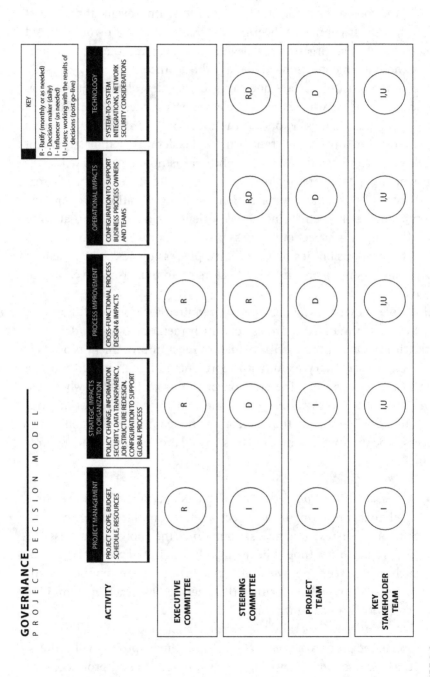

FIGURE 3.3
Project governance decision model.

cases, the process owner will be a leader on the project, but many times, he or she is simply a contributing member of the team.

- *Project leads*: Project leaders usually include the project manager and one or more business or technical leaders who help to drive the project forward from a productivity and staffing standpoint.
- *Executive committee*: The executive committee is the highest level of oversight in a company's governance structure and is the driving force behind our organization's strategic plan. It reviews the performance of the organization against its strategic objectives and receives regular updates with regard to projects and programs, issues and risks, and other related variables, including status, project scope, budget, schedules, and timelines. It defines the overall strategy and direction, along with enterprise targets, and provides guidance to program teams accordingly.
- *Steering committee*: The steering committee receives overall direction from the strategies outlined by the executive committee. It ensures optimal sequencing of activities, and steers projects and programs in a positive manner as they relate to the broader enterprise strategy. It is a group of high-level stakeholders in an organization that act as an advising committee regarding projects and other efforts. The steering committee may be responsible for selecting projects, assigning teams, and overseeing projects with regard to budgets and timelines.
- *Core and extended project teams*: The core and extended project teams are responsible for delivery of daily project activities and actions. They regularly report on project status, issues, risks, open decisions, and dependencies. These individuals should also be comprised of process users who work directly with the process. Be sure to select an appropriate sample, not just those who execute the process well. Team members should be given the needed authority, and the responsibility to fully execute the improvement project. From the beginning of a project, all members need to be made aware of what is expected of them. Because the project team will have members from across the company representing a variety of job functions and skill sets, the project leads need to ensure that all team members have the tools that they require to be successful. If an individual has not been a member of an improvement team in the past, the manager will have to assess what additional training needs to be provided to ensure he has the skills and confidence necessary to be a valuable contributor to the process.

- *Subject matter experts (SMEs)*: Experienced or skilled employees of any level who provide information or guidance to the team. SMEs may be full project participants or may be involved only as needed to provide information.
- *Coordinator*: A full-time project participant who is elected to take notes at all meetings and provide those notes to participants. Project leads sometimes take on this role, but it isn't recommended, as it's difficult to take comprehensive notes while leading a meeting or group exercise. The coordinator is a full-time project participant who is elected to ensure meetings remain agenda focused and on time.
- *Technology expert*: Technology plays a large role in just about any process improvement initiative today. Having access to key systems developers or SMEs can be quite valuable when designing solutions and determining root causes.
- *Stakeholders*: All other individuals contributing to the team effort or who have a vested interest in its outcomes.

A core project team consisting of six to eight members is ideal. More team members can slow progress, and too few may not provide the input and resource power to complete tasks in a reasonable time frame. A team leader must be appointed and will schedule and conduct meetings and manage the process improvement effort. All team members should be closely involved in the process and participate in decisions, discussions, data collection, and any analysis activities. Team members should attend all meetings and complete preparatory work as assigned. The time requirements of a team member are dependent on the process being analyzed or the improvement being proposed.

Obtain Project Charter and Scope Approval

Obtaining scope approval starts with providing a project charter to key stakeholders for their review and endorsement, allowing any needed executives and stakeholders the opportunity to provide feedback. It is beneficial to provide an opportunity for discussion in order to ensure there is adequate awareness and consensus on the project and its scope.

Other Planning Activities

Other planning activities may include

- *Deciding project status and review schedules*: Determine appropriate timing for reviewing the project and verifying its effectiveness. This must be an ongoing effort to enable continual support and success.
- *Determining ground rules*: Establish ground rules for how the project will be executed, including how team members will solve conflicts, how issues will be escalated, and how project status will be reported and communicated.
- *Determining process and project change controls*: As the need to change process or project scope arises, it must be done in a managed and deliberate way. Any changes must be agreed upon by stakeholders, and the process or project scope changes must be documented and approved.
- *Collecting process maps and documents*: It is important to collect any process maps and companion documents as process improvement efforts kick off in order to not waste time and energy recreating duplicate artifacts.

Analyzing

Now that the process improvement initiative is fully planned, it's time to move to the analyze phase, where the problem areas in questions will be assessed. Once the team is established, they must fully understand the process they will be improving. The analyze phase involves gathering pertinent information about the process in question and how it operates in its current state.

Mapping exercises also let teams identify roles and discover critical metrics. After deciding on metrics, teams may also gather data for statistical analysis or to help them validate assumptions about the process. Teams begin to brainstorm solutions and select the solution that best solves the problem they are working on.

Key deliverables in this phase include

- A process map or maps of current processes (documenting the way work flows through the process)
- A list of disconnects and pain points
- Baseline metrics
- Benchmarking on how other firms handle the process

Conduct Project Kickoff

Conduct the project kickoff meeting and provide an overview to the team and relevant stakeholders on methodology, approach, timing, ground rules, and other initiation criteria.

Facilitate Process Discovery

Process discovery helps identify why and for whom the process exists, what its purpose is, and how it operates in its current state. Process discovery may involve several techniques that lead to scope validation or reveal the need to change scope. These include

- *Capturing high-level processes*: A SIPOC (suppliers, inputs, process, outputs, customers) is a visual tool used to illustrate the high-level flow of a process, customers of the process, and the suppliers, inputs, and outputs.
- *Reviewing existing process documentation*: Locate existing documentation about the process for general information purposes and gather process maps prior to interviews if available.
- *Conducting interviews*: Meet with operators who are involved in the process or with stakeholders who ultimately care about it. This could include supervisors, peers, employees, customers, management, or suppliers. In simple terms, ask them what they think works well, what doesn't, and document any suggestions they may have for improvement. Some tips for conducting successful interviews are as follows:
  - Develop an interview questionnaire to ensure consistent and key points are covered in the interviews and determine how interview information will be captured and summarized.
  - Determine the personnel to interview in conjunction with the assigned SMEs. Be sure to talk with process owners and other key personnel who perform the process, personnel who integrate with the process, and any customers of the process.
  - Schedule and conduct the interviews during key working hours and summarize and send recaps of the results.
- *Walking the process*: Observe process personnel as they perform the process and validate that the process map contains all the pertinent activities, tasks, and interfaces. You may also discover other steps are involved, as well as other people, other tools, or other interfaces used that should be captured in the process map.

SIPOC (sometimes COPIS) is a tool that summarizes the inputs and outputs of one or more processes in table form. The acronym SIPOC stands for suppliers, inputs, process, outputs, and customers, which form the columns of the table.

Document and Analyze Current State

This phase maps the current state in detail and establishes its current baseline and measurement with an eye toward showing current process value versus waste. Analyze the current state process or processes against identified issues, concerns, and pain points. Look for areas of inefficiency. When you map the process you want to improve, you document all of the activities that occur when the process is under way. In order to document a current state process, you must gather data on all aspects of it, including how many transactions there are, who is involved, how often it takes place, and how long it takes to execute. Ultimately, documenting and analyzing a process may involve several activities:

- Creating process maps. A process map is a valuable tool for understanding the process with a visual representation. It helps identify opportunities to enhance value, eliminate waste, and improve the flow of a process. Description documents or process profiles for each of the process maps are beneficial to various target audiences who do not need to know the level of detail in a map. Keys to successfully mapping a process include the next steps.
- Conducting mapping sessions with the SMEs. These sessions are iterative as process details are uncovered and reviewed for accuracy. Create a process profile document that captures process details that the model does not capture.
- Identify the organizations that perform the process; key activities performed; roles, departments, and people involved in the process; tools or systems used; interfaces with other processes; and so forth.
- Determine timing and constraints of the process and identify measures currently used to manage the process.
- Determine process problems, disconnects, or pain points and identify a variety of solutions to improve the process. Brainstorm with colleagues and consult SMEs, looking at root causes, and consider practical applications to the obvious problems. Recognize where root causes are not understood and whether a final recommendation

for more in-depth analysis is warranted. Be sure to examine each component of the process and gather all feedback regarding problems or pain points. Asking questions such as the following helps vet out most issues: Where does the process experience delay? What is most frustrating about the process? Which areas take unreasonably long amounts of time to complete? Are there quality issues? Are there gaps in time between activities? Always ensure true root causes are identified so you do not implement a fix that in reality breaks other parts of the process or does not get to the true issue at hand. Other common pain points or waste areas include

- Large amounts of information exchanged between workers, data duplication, or redundant data entry
- Rework and multiple iterations of work
- Large amounts of checking and inspection
- Excess complexity and special procedures in a process
- Excess inventory, work in progress, or buffers

- Validate process maps and documents. Review documentation captured about the process and verify current state validity and measurements.
- Collect and analyze data. Gather and review data required to measure the process and review the measures to ensure valid results. Analyze and discuss data with other process performers and process team members as appropriate, and compare the measurements with the expected results with the goals and objectives for the process. Types of data associated with process improvement projects usually include
  - Customers of the process (internal or external to the company)
  - Suppliers to the process
  - Key deliverables or outputs of the process
  - Key receivables or inputs of the process
  - Timing information for the activities that make up the process
  - Cost information
  - Resource information (personnel and equipment used to perform a process)
  - Fallout, reject, and rework information
- Identify process needs and changes. Determine whether the process requires updates, analysis, or additional effort. Brainstorm solutions and decide which solutions for each of the pain points and which changes you will move forward with.

Benchmarking is a very useful exercise that is often forgotten when conducting process improvements. Determining how other organizations execute similar processes can help bring about a clear advantage. Ensure your benchmarking includes examining how the process in question is performed by competitors or other industry leaders, and ask how they have solved similar problems in the past.

Present Current State Findings

Summarize, document, and review all the findings from analysis and share these results with key stakeholders. Share how the existing process truly operates and whether the current state is in line with the original objectives of the process. Indicate obvious areas of waste where there may be improvement potential for reducing cost or increasing value to process customers.

Obtain Approval

Prepare a summary of findings for purposes of formal process review and evaluation.

If no additional process analysis is needed, be sure to get approval to continue on to the next phase. If approval is not obtained, continue process analysis until all pain points have been addressed and root causes identified and bring the results back for review and evaluation.

Designing

During the design phase, teams create the new process or make changes to the existing process according to the solution or solutions they selected in the previous stage. They select the specific improvements to the process that will be proposed, document what this process will look like in the future, identify additional process controls and measures as needed, and outline a road map to move the process to the newly proposed state. The results of this phase determine whether a process improvement recommendation will be fully undertaken. This phase also involves mapping the new process and creating documentation, including any detailed procedures and training materials, to prepare for the implementation phase. Process mapping is an essential tool during this phase, because it lets you see how the new process will play out within the organization and identify any potential risks or issues that will be created by the change. You can also test or pilot changes in this phase if needed as well.

What Is Delivered during This Phase?

- A process map of the future state of the process
- Risk assessments
- Recommendations for improvements
- Test scenarios and results
- An implementation plan

Document Future State

Determine the proposed future state process from the set of potential process improvements. Document the proposed future state process in models as appropriate. Document process controls, measurements, and any other process components. Here, the main goal is to visualize what an ideal process would look like, being sure that it directly addresses the problems identified. Other future state considerations may include

- Required compliance criteria: Make sure that the process factors in requirements for any policies and regulations that are required by law.
- Best practices: As you implement the process, apply known best practices and communicate them to all involved in process operations.
- Procedures: Implementation requires detailed task-level instructions and specific requirements for some steps. Be sure that any required steps are clearly defined and documented.

Conduct Refinements

Further gauge the feasibility and results of the redesigned process by discussing various process, organization, and human ramifications. Depending on the nature of the changes, you may determine your process needs further changes. Be sure to consider ways to further improve as well, such as assessing whether any further costs could be reduced. Could any additional steps be eliminated from the process to reduce the number of resources required? Other areas to verify include

- Can the cycle time be reduced any further in the new process?
- Has customer satisfaction been improved in the new process?

- Has quality been improved in the new process?
- Does the newly designed process address the performance issues and pain points described by stakeholders?
- Are there any areas in the new process that could cause other issues within the process or with other processes?
- Will the new process require new jobs or roles to be created, or will any be removed?
- Will the new process require training employees on new sills or hiring new employees with specific skill sets?
- Will the new process require any human resources (HR) involvement or specific communications?
- Will the new process require any new systems to be purchased or built or enhancements to infrastructure?

Test Ideas

The project team along with stakeholders will likely feel very passionately about its proposed solutions. After designing solutions and proposed changes, test them to ensure optimal results and applicability to the business environment. This can be done through various means, such as role-playing, where team members act out the proposed process to see how well it works. Another way is to take real-life scenarios and practice executing them with the new way of working, pausing when issues may arise and reassessing the solution and tweaking as practice runs are executed. Lastly, advanced tools like modeling suites have simulation capabilities built in. Here, team members can populate data and various scenarios into the tool to find bottlenecks and other problems and verify the results of the process, including whether existing pain points have been addressed and if new ones have been created. Testing helps ensure corrections are ideal and is a fairly low-cost way of ensuring success.

Process simulation is an instrument for the analysis of business processes. It is used to assess the dynamic behavior of processes over time, e.g., the development of process and resource performance in reaction to changes or fluctuations of certain environment or system parameters. The results provide insights to support decisions in process design or resource provision with the goal to improve factors such as process performance, process and product quality, customer satisfaction, or resource utilization.

Identify Resources

Now that a future state process has been designed, it is time to identify and obtain the resources needed to put the newly designed process into action. Regardless of the changes, this may require working with many different groups across the company, including HR, IT, and finance.

Along with human resources, be sure to cover other resourcing areas, such as

- Whether new equipment or technology is needed
- Whether new physical space is needed
- Whether adequate technology support from IT is in place
- Whether new management responsibilities are needed

Of course, many process changes are minor and do not require such substantial resourcing, but always be sure that all needed resources are identified and acquired before beginning your implementation.

Conduct Readiness Assessment

Determine whether process participants are ready to implement the proposed changes. Some considerations include

- What is the organization's willingness to adopt the process changes?
- What is the organization's ability to do the work to implement the process?
- Do the recommended improvements require significant change by those performing the process?
- What is the willingness to assign an active process owner?

Present Future State

Typically, the project team then presents the final recommendations to key stakeholders. Keep in mind that stakeholders tend to prefer a high-level overview rather than detailed reports. Prepare your presentation from a high-level perspective, but be prepared to answer questions in depth. Areas to cover include

- *Scope and goals*: Be sure to include a reminder of the original scope and objectives that were agreed upon in the planning phase to provide context for the remainder of the presentation.

- *Current state findings*: Provide a brief review of the major findings and discoveries obtained during the analyze phase.
- *Future state recommendations*: Outline any future state recommendations and solutions, providing rationale for each. Identify those that require approval before continuing to implementation and which ones are quick wins versus those that require significant time and investment.
- *Timeline and estimates*: Always be sure to provide clear steps for implementing recommended solutions. Indicate the estimated maturity level and new operating environment for the target state and be sure to outline any dependencies and perceived risks of implementing or not implementing the solutions.
- *Resource requirements*: Outline needed resource requirements to implement any of the proposed solutions, improvements, or fixes.

Changing processes and accompanying mindsets can be challenging. To help assist with this transition, always ensure changes to the process continue to enhance the value provided to the customers of the process. Ensure future state designs are not constrained by job titles or current organizational structure and involve HR as needed. Attack the biggest time wasters or pain points first, and look for opportunities to remove any unnecessary activities that could decrease the number of steps or simply steps that may be overly complex. Keeping things Lean in focus and design thinking will help ensure a successful improvement implementation.

Implementing

During implementation, actual changes are made to the process or a new process is put into action. This phase refers to the final process of moving the proposed solutions from the development state to the production state. Depending on your project, this process is often called deployment, go-live, rollout, or even installation. All of these terms are synonymous with implementation. As with most change efforts, there is no single way to implement a new process or process changes. It depends on the characteristics of your improvement effort and the proposed transformation. Some implementations are as easy as just doing it, where implementation is just a state of mind or very low effort or complexity.

At the other end of the spectrum, implementations may become projects in and of themselves. For instance, you may have a software application that needs to be deployed to various departments. This could take weeks or months to accomplish. In this case, you might structure the implementation as a separate project.

When you think about implementation, you should always start by understanding the level of complexity involved and any obstacles that may hinder success. If the implementation is relatively straightforward, then there is no reason for elaborate implementation processes. However, most projects have a number of implementation events to plan for and execute successfully.

What is delivered during this phase?

- Training materials
- Process and procedure documentation
- A method for monitoring the process
- A definition for continued success of the process

Understand Obstacles

Before implementing your new process, it's beneficial to understand common obstacles to implementing the redesign and determining what steps you and the team will take to avoid them. Common obstacles include resistance from employees, resistance from managers, no management support, lack of awareness, lack of involvement, and lack of resources.

Secure Needed Process Roles

Confirm commitment and involvement from those who perform roles pertaining to the process, including the process owner or process manager, business process analyst, SMEs, and process performers.

Obtain and Prepare Technology Changes

Some process changes may require software or equipment changes. Obtaining and preparing the tools that are necessary to implement the process may be conducted during the setup process.

Prepare Production Turnover Plan

Establish a plan for expanding the process to production.

Decide Process Verification and Review Schedule

Determine appropriate timing for reviewing the process and verifying its effectiveness. This must be an ongoing effort to enable continual improvement.

Determine Process Change Control

As needs arise to change the process, it must be done in a managed and deliberate way. Future changes must be agreed upon by key stakeholders.

Update Process Maps and Document

As changes are applied to the process, it is important to update process maps and their companion documents accordingly.

Plan Training and Education

Before implementing the new process, those who perform process activities must learn the new steps or activities. Be sure to design training or support materials and ensure proper training sessions are scheduled and any needed communications are rolled out.

Deploy Process

Roll out the new process official to process owners and participants. This includes officially announcing the new process changes and providing any needed hypercare or support as it goes live.

Remove Past Artifacts

Remove any artifacts of the old process to reduce temptation to shift back to old ways of working or causing unnecessary confusion. These artifacts may include old forms, old process maps, old signage, and old procedures. Removing these sends a message of support for the new way of working.

Document Lessons Learned

Project teams should conduct a review of their improvement initiatives for the purposes of honing individual or group skills or for suggesting refinements to the process improvement framework. Here the purpose is to measure the effectiveness of the framework itself. Retrospectives are an excellent way to gather feedback and outline what went well, what didn't, and where things could be improved on the next improvement initiative.

Transition Project

Transition is usually the final step in any process improvement project. Successful improvements do not remain forever in a project environment— final success is seen when the improved process transitions back to regular management and day-to-day functions. Regular teams can't always give the same type of attention to the process as the project team did, as they are busy keeping up with productivity. A transition plan helps regular teams operate and evaluate the process. One of the best ways project teams can do this is to provide business areas with easy-to-use monitors. Control charts and other graphical representations are often the best monitors, as teams don't have to analyze data themselves. An automated dashboard of charts lets department leaders keep an eye on the process and understand almost immediately when something may be out of control.

Continuously Improving

Now that you've implemented your process changes, you must ensure that those changes continue to deliver the results required. Sustained organizational change is brought about by the cumulative impact of all individuals' efforts to continually improve themselves, their jobs, and their organization. During the continuous improvement phase, the focus is on the ongoing improvement of the skills and behaviors of the individuals involved in the process, which form the foundation of ongoing process improvement. In order for a process improvement to be successful, there must be ongoing governing and managing elements in place to ensure continuous improvement, such as

- Determining a suitable cadence to review process performance.
- Measuring the process performance.
- Revising performance metrics as needed.
- Continually identifying issues, looking for improvement opportunities, and taking any needed action.
- Updating expectations and targets as needed.

- Monitoring process compliance.
- Providing process production support.
- Ensuring appropriate process user training.
- Addressing process user performance issues.
- Creating constancy of purpose toward improvement of product and service, with the aim to become competitive, stay in business, and provide jobs.
- Instituting training on the job.
- Instituting leadership. The aim of supervision should be to help people and machines and gadgets to do a better job.
- Driving out fear so that everyone may work effectively for the company.
- Breaking down barriers between departments. People in research, design, sales, and production must work as a team to foresee problems of production and use of the product or service. Process improvement is everybody's job.
- Instituting a vigorous program of education and self-improvement.

Take Needed Action to Improve

Process improvement is a system to make people think differently. It is not just about building improved processes, nor is it simply about developing powerful tools that increase value and eliminate waste. Above all, process improvement represents a radical change in thinking. Managers and employees frame all their activities in disciplined ways and constantly reflect upon and improve how they are producing value. Ultimately, process improvement can be characterized as managing work in a new way, determining better ways of working, and constantly problem solving.

All improvement starts with people. The first step is to engage with your employees by leading with respect, creating a meaningful challenge, and fostering a workplace where process excellence is the norm. When you engage with people respectfully, they respond in ways you never could have dreamed plausible.

In a process improvement framework, we encourage engaging those closest to the work to define a target state, determine current status, measure the gaps, and identify roadblocks and obstacles. A process improvement framework also ensures proper testing to strengthen understanding of cause and effect and validates which countermeasures effectively move the dial and achieve measureable results. Once a project is completed, though, this thinking process is one that does not stop. As part of the implement phase, proper transition includes handing over the tools needed to frequently repeat the process until it becomes embedded into daily work routines. Although it seems straightforward and relatively simple, if process performance falls short of targets, you and your team must decide what, if any, actions are needed to address the shortfalls. When team members constantly explore ideas for improvement action, they are truly working with a process improvement mindset.

CLOSING REMARKS

A corporation without a proper management framework is like a train without a track. No matter how much potential the business has, it will never undergo the business transformation needed to get to where it wants because it has nothing directing its progress. Undertaking a process improvement project can be a big adventure for those involved, but if they are approached with a structured plan, enthusiasm, and management support, they will often reap great benefits. Although there is no one way to approach managing change, numerous methodologies have developed over the years, and all of them have common phases that help align process improvement efforts across a company. Establishing a common process improvement framework at your company helps bring meaningful purpose, practical strategies, and goals together, ultimately making your organization's aspirations more credible and more likely to be achieved.

Implementing a process improvement framework requires time and thought from committed leaders who understand the benefits of aligning every level of an organization to produce desired results and continuously improve itself. It ensures that a business environment is fair and transparent and that employees can be held accountable for their actions. Conversely, a weak framework can lead to waste, mismanagement, and even corruption. Regardless of the type of company, only a solid process improvement framework with proper governance can deliver sustainable and improved business performance. Together, these bring deeper meaning and tangible progress, while also cementing trust within the organization as it delivers more efficiently for customers, enables its people to lead, and discovers better ways of working. Organizations that demonstrate discipline, earn and keep trust, and establish boundaries and standards are those that can continue improving indefinitely.

4

Process Architecture

Many companies, both large and small, have initiated some form of business process improvement strategy. These strategies have taken many different forms, from requiring individual business units or departments to document processes, to enterprise-wide recognition of the importance of aligning business processes with the financial and operational goals of the organization. At one end of the spectrum, numerous binders detailing work processes sit atop cubicle desks, while at the other end, automated tools are used to structure, maintain, and integrate business processes with the daily execution of business activities. How an organization stores and manages information about its business processes presents a clue as to whether they are considered nice-to-have artifacts or true business assets. Uncontrolled growth of process information can lead to unclear structures, duplicate or missing information, and redundant or failed improvements.

Having a well-organized process architecture that is clearly understood across the organization, is linked to key corporate strategies, and is managed on a day-to-day basis is key to overcoming this barrier. When everyone has the same understanding of strategy, and how processes are connected and contribute to that strategy, process activities become synergized and productivity improves dramatically. This chapter describes the basics of process architecture and how it helps bridge gaps between technical and business resources and helps people take an enterprise-level approach to process improvement.

By the end of this chapter, you should be able to

- Define process architecture
- Explain the benefits and key attributes of process architecture

- Describe the difference between process architecture and other related constructs
- Define process-oriented architecture (POA)
- State the definition of process modeling
- Outline the various types of modeling notations
- List several process analysis and management tools

WHAT IS PROCESS ARCHITECTURE?

Inside every company is a core set of systems and processes that execute the thousands of daily transactions that keep it in business, such as taking orders, purchasing supplies, delivering products, and paying employees. The way these processes are structured can help or hinder its efforts to execute its strategy. For an organization to function effectively, it is vital that it understand the structure of all of the business processes that exist and create value within its organization. Within any given company, hundreds, or even thousands or millions, of processes exist in order for daily operations to occur. How these processes integrate, communicate, and work together toward overall business goals is governed by process architecture.

We define process architecture as the design and organization of business processes and related components into a unified structure and hierarchy. It provides an overview of the various process systems, interfaces, interdependencies, rules, and other relationships within and between processes across a company, and helps align functional business objectives and strategies to process execution. When an organization seriously engages in architecting its business processes and looks at itself through various perspectives, inevitably questions arise. Which processes exist in my organization? How are they connected? At what level of detail should we map our processes? Where does one process end and another begin? Which processes are redundant or possess waste? By formulating an enterprise-wide perspective that cuts across departments, and business processes, process architecture ensures that an organization's goals and objectives are addressed in a holistic way across the entire enterprise. Having a business process architecture strategy in place can create a vital, unifying principle for successfully creating, introducing, using, improving, and maintaining organizational processes and ensuring all processes contribute to organizational goals and strategies.

> Process components, also known as process elements, describe the various units of a process. Examples of process components include departments, systems, data elements, people, systems, information, artifacts, inputs, outputs, triggers, goals, and relationships—just about anything that can interact with a process or that is related to a process. Modeling these components and structuring them into a suitable hierarchy, tagging them for easy navigation, and enabling proper search capabilities allows users to connect easily with the process information they care about (Figure 4.1).

There are several key features a capable process architecture is going to need to support the organization and manage all of its content and complexity. Key principles of process architecture include (Figure 4.2):

1. *Iterative*: Process architecture is not a waterfall approach. Each iteration of the model provides more insight into a company's business environment and its business problems, and potential solutions for addressing those issues become progressively more detailed and apparent over time. As a result, with process architecture, one does not need to know every process detail in order to move ideas forward, but just enough to make the next decision.

2. *Reusable*: Process architecture is not a one-time analysis of a business environment. Rather, it provides a foundation for current and future analysis and decision making. Unless an organization has changed significantly, through acquisition, for example, the existing process architecture model and all of its components should be used as the starting point for future efforts.

3. *Not prescriptive*: There are no two organizations or business situations that are exactly alike. This means that the same process architecture deliverables and techniques cannot be employed in every situation.

4. *Information rich*: An organization's process architecture should be capable of managing the full set of information required to define and manage its processes and related entities and artifacts. Processes, steps, roles, risks, products, and events are just a few of the types of entities that may be used to assist in the definition of a process.

5. *Relationally rich*: Along with the complex relationships contained within a process, processes have many relationships to other

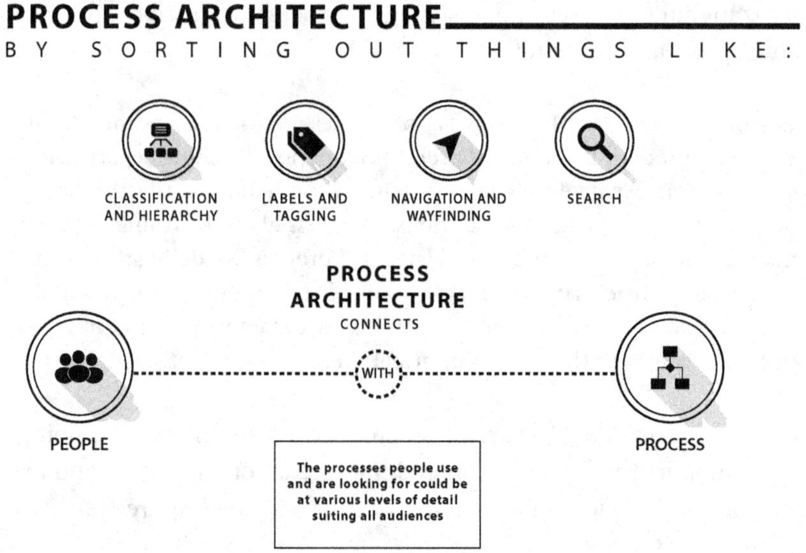

PROCESS ARCHITECTURE

B Y   S O R T I N G   O U T   T H I N G S   L I K E :

CLASSIFICATION
AND HIERARCHY

LABELS AND
TAGGING

NAVIGATION AND
WAYFINDING

SEARCH

**PROCESS
ARCHITECTURE**
CONNECTS

PEOPLE

WITH

PROCESS

The processes people use
and are looking for could be
at various levels of detail
suiting all audiences

FIGURE 4.1
Process architecture overview.

important processes and components across a company. Process assets, policies, measures, systems, data, performance baselines, and any transitional models are just a few of the external entities that may have complex relationships with processes.

6. *Analytically rich*: The ability for process architecture to support analysis is central to process improvement efforts at higher levels of maturity and capability. Selection of processes by performance objectives and their composition into a meaningful whole can be of particular use.

7. *Presentation rich*: Process architecture exists to be used, and not everyone who uses it is a process expert. Therefore, complex information and relationships have to be presented effectively to process users and operators to ensure that full and effective use is made of the process architecture and its content. Only then can all of the benefits of the investment in structuring and organizing processes be achieved and recognized.

Process architecture is much harder to implement than most imagine. Very few employees can describe the connection between corporate strategies and the work their department performs. It takes an organized and concerted effort to turn high-level strategy into meaningful action. However, when process architecture is defined, its use imposes a degree of overhead on the organization, and the content of the architecture has to be used and

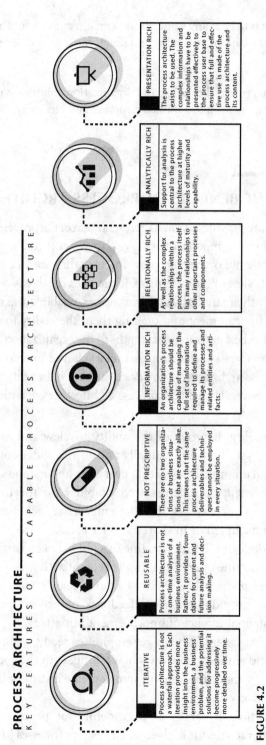

PROCESS ARCHITECTURE
KEY FEATURES OF A CAPABLE PROCESS ARCHITECTURE

ITERATIVE

Process architecture is not a waterfall approach. Each iteration provides more insight into the business environment, a business problem, and the potential solutions for addressing it become progressively more detailed over time.

REUSABLE

Process architecture is not a one-time analysis of a business environment. Rather, it provides a foundation for current and future analysis and decision making.

NOT PRESCRIPTIVE

There are no two organizations or business situations that are exactly alike. This means that the same process architecture deliverables and techniques cannot be employed in every situation.

INFORMATION RICH

An organization's process architecture should be capable of managing the full set of information required to define and manage its processes and related entities and artifacts.

RELATIONALLY RICH

As well as the complex relationships within a process, the process itself has many relationships to other important processes and components.

ANALYTICALLY RICH

Support for analysis is central to the process architecture at higher levels of maturity and capability.

PRESENTATION RICH

The process architecture exists to be used. The complex information and relationships have to be presented effectively to the process user base to ensure that full and effective use is made of the process architecture and its content.

FIGURE 4.2

Key features of a capable process architecture.

maintained if it is to have any value. Process architecture should be seen to provide benefits to the organization, and if not, can lead to failed improvement efforts.

 Process Architecture is the design and organization of business processes and related components into a unified structure and hierarchy.

WHAT ARE THE BENEFITS OF PROCESS ARCHITECTURE?

Process architecture provides a visual representation of the processes and process systems within a company, offering executives and employees a bird's-eye view of the activities of the enterprise and how they are all connected. By gaining an overall view of the enterprise, it becomes much easier for organizations to identify their strengths and weaknesses, enabling them to identify areas in need of improvement and offering them the ability to develop the strategies needed to best exploit the strengths of the organization. In addition to aligning perspectives and efforts across all levels and functions in a business, proper process architecture provides a number of benefits to organizations and people. Several benefits of process architecture are outlined below:

- *Process visibility*: It provides the ability to view and analyze end-to-end processes both individually and in the wider context of the enterprise in an intuitive way that everyone understands.
- *Process ownership*: It ensures accountability for the improvement of end-to-end processes across the enterprise, including extended activities outsourced or in shared service areas.
- *Strategic alignment*: It provides line of sight between corporate strategies and frontline operational improvement activities.
- *Performance metrics*: It embeds key performance indicators within processes to provide immediate feedback on process performance, and the potential impact of improvement initiatives.
- *Change management*: It helps get employees ready, willing, and able to accept and embrace new ways of working, with the goal of involving people in the improvement journey, not just imposing process transformation on them.
- *Standardization*: It serves as a guideline for process analysts to devise best practices for high-level and basic processes to ensure that

all processes are aligned with the overall business strategy and are formatted and structured in a common fashion.

- *Automation opportunities*: It helps to identify processes, or activities within processes, that could be effectively automated to reduce the burden on staff members, as well as increase speed and efficiency.
- *Simplification*: It enables process architectures to highlight redundant and complicated processes, allowing management to improve those areas and streamline the business.
- *Reduced cost*: The simplification and automation of processes should, ideally, result in reduced operational costs for the enterprise.
- *Training benefits*: These provide a visual representation of the processes and procedures of an enterprise and can be a powerful training tool for new staff, or retraining existing staff. By using process architecture models, it is possible to reduce training and ramp time.
- *Faster reactions*: Simplification and increased automation should also result in quicker reaction to changing market conditions, allowing executives to quickly adapt existing processes to new conditions.
- *Strategy creation*: A comprehensive overview of the processes across a company can be an invaluable aid in the creation and adjustment of business strategies. By using process architecture to identify strengths and core competencies, executives can determine how to best move the enterprise forward.
- *Costing*: A company's process architectures can assist with highlighting areas of waste, and where process outputs do not justify investment. These processes can then be remodeled or eliminated. Process architectures can also predict the cost of alterations to processes.
- *Impact prediction*: Lastly, process architectures can offer managers insight into how processes interrelate, and how modifications to any one process may affect downstream or synchronized processes. By understanding the impact a process change will have on its surrounding processes, executives can determine the best course of action for the improvement.

To be successful, process architecture should be woven into company culture and embedded into the life cycle of the organization, including capital planning, project management, process improvement, resource allocation, and strategy formulation. Everyone thinking about how they fit into the larger company construct is critical toward sustaining the overall enterprise model.

WHAT IS THE DIFFERENCE BETWEEN PROCESS ARCHITECTURE AND OTHER ARCHITECTURES?

Process architecture is not quite the same thing as system, business, or data architecture, although all four concepts are related and certainly have similarities under the broader enterprise architecture discipline. Systems architecture applies the same concepts of integration and communication, but is usually limited to the world of technology. Data architecture is concerned with how data are stored, managed, secured, integrated, archived, accessed, and used. Business architecture is usually concerned with connecting strategy and tactical business functions.

All four pillars of architecture—process, business, systems, and data—work together to form the enterprise architecture for an organization. In most cases, the architectures don't actually exist separately, but are considered as such in order to break down functionality and responsibility, as seen in Figure 4.3.

All of the various forms of architecture can be used to address the same problems or organizational goals from different viewpoints. Process architecture might be concerned with how labor can be aligned with production goals for optimal success, or how to create and integrate workflows to improve production, for example. Systems architecture could be applied to visualize how current hardware, systems, applications, and networks can be deployed to support the processes, and data architecture lays out how information is used within the process.

WHAT IS PROCESS-ORIENTED ARCHITECTURE?

In isolation, process architecture is about the way processes are structured, described, and interrelated. For organizations working toward higher levels of maturity and capability, their process architecture does not exist in isolation. It exists in the context of a family of organizational assets, which support the definition, deployment, use, and improvement of processes throughout the organization. POA occurs when all other architectures are centralized on the process of things rather than the specific business, service, data, or technology architecture. Although driven by process, POA is a model that strives to unify all architectures into one framework for optimal efficiency and understanding of an organization.

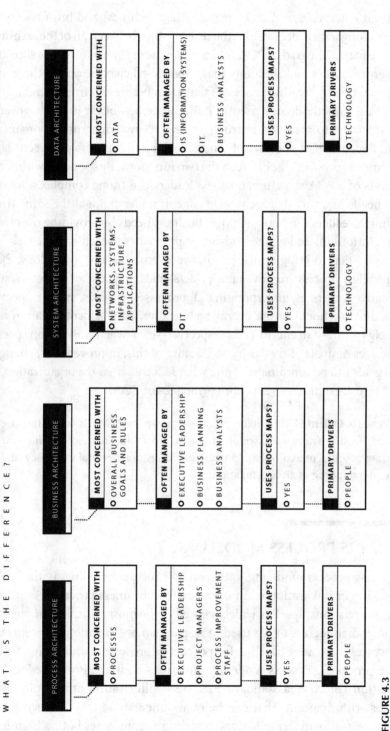

ARCHITECTURE TYPES

WHAT IS THE DIFFERENCE?

FIGURE 4.3
Four pillars of architecture.

At an enterprise level, POA occurs when technical and business structures, along with processes and the relationships between all of these things, are the focus. The goal of POA is to tear down traditional business silos and design resources and solutions that enhance efficiencies across the entire organization by creating processes that are reusable and interoperable.

POA is a methodology used to build processes, but it is also a governing structure to maintain a strong process ecosystem across an organization. Because POA speaks to both technical and business perspectives, it becomes a sort of bridge between the two functions. By speaking within the bounds of a POA structure, business leaders can frame complex solutions and needs in a way that technical staff can understand; at the same time, technical leaders can better support business needs by providing overarching solutions instead of one-and-done approaches to each specific task.

In addition to bridging the gap between business and technology, POA helps align process improvement professionals, day-to-day operators, and executive leaders. By incorporating all processes, projects, systems, people, data, and functions into one overall architecture, management can always see the big picture—an end-to-end perspective—even when working on specific processes or areas of the business. Because of this, improvements, changes, and goals can be coordinated, enhancing success across the organization.

Figure 4.4 outlines the six core principles of POA.

 Process-Oriented Architecture, also known as POA, is an enterprise architecture framework which strives to unify all architecture into one framework centered on the process of things, for optimal efficiency and understanding of an organization.

WHAT IS PROCESS MODELING?

Business process modeling, often called process modeling, is the representation or illustration of an organization's business processes and their various relationships. It is widely viewed as the most critical component in process architecture and is used to map out an organization's current state processes to create a baseline for process improvement and design future state processes. Process modeling often uses Business Process Modeling Notation (BPMN), a standard method of illustrating or mapping processes with diagrams that can be easily understood by both technology and business managers. Process modeling encompasses both a high-level

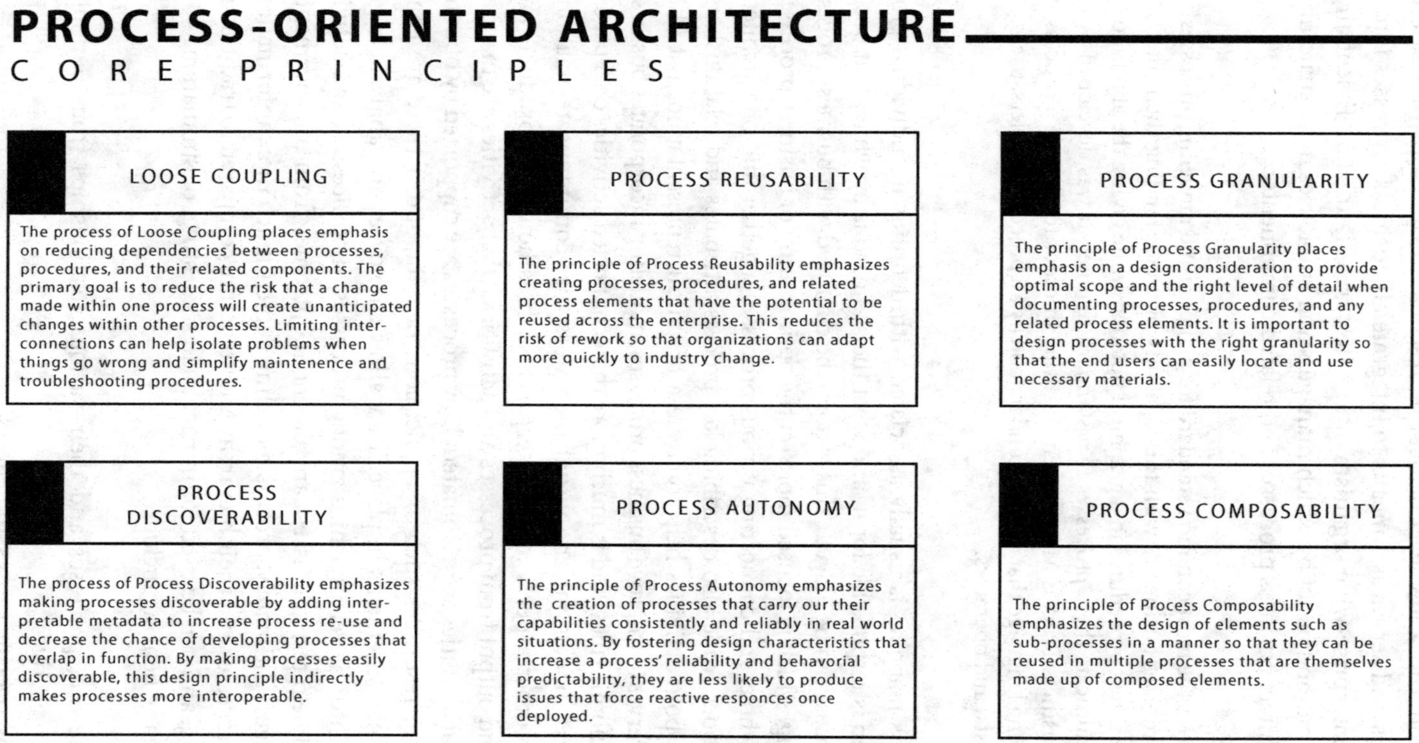

PROCESS-ORIENTED ARCHITECTURE
C O R E   P R I N C I P L E S

LOOSE COUPLING

The process of Loose Coupling places emphasis on reducing dependencies between processes, procedures, and their related components. The primary goal is to reduce the risk that a change made within one process will create unanticipated changes within other processes. Limiting inter-connections can help isolate problems when things go wrong and simplify maintenence and troubleshooting procedures.

PROCESS DISCOVERABILITY

The process of Process Discoverability emphasizes making processes discoverable by adding inter-pretable metadata to increase process re-use and decrease the chance of developing processes that overlap in function. By making processes easily discoverable, this design principle indirectly makes processes more interoperable.

PROCESS REUSABILITY

The principle of Process Reusability emphasizes creating processes, procedures, and related process elements that have the potential to be reused across the enterprise. This reduces the risk of rework so that organizations can adapt more quickly to industry change.

PROCESS AUTONOMY

The principle of Process Autonomy emphasizes the creation of processes that carry our their capabilities consistently and reliably in real world situations. By fostering design characteristics that increase a process' reliability and behavorial predictability, they are less likely to produce issues that force reactive responces once deployed.

PROCESS GRANULARITY

The principle of Process Granularity places emphasis on a design consideration to provide optimal scope and the right level of detail when documenting processes, procedures, and any related process elements. It is important to design processes with the right granularity so that the end users can easily locate and use necessary materials.

PROCESS COMPOSABILITY

The principle of Process Composability emphasizes the design of elements such as sub-processes in a manner so that they can be reused in multiple processes that are themselves made up of composed elements.

FIGURE 4.4
Core principles of POA.

adaptation and a low-level tactical representation of any of the various processes and serves as a means to integrate all business processes into a single, enterprise-wide organism or architecture (Figure 4.5). Essentially, it is the method or act by which managers and employees map, structure, and architect business processes and related components.

 BPMN is the most common standard for mapping and modeling processes and provides businesses with the capability of understanding their internal business procedures in a graphical notation while giving the ability to communicate these processes in a standard manner. It was developed by the Business Process Management Institute in order to provide a process mapping language that could be understood by all process modelers, users, analysts, and operators.

Process mapping is usually associated with defining an individual process, who is responsible for it, and what the standard is by which that business process can be judged. This is not to be confused with business process modeling, which is focused more on the optimization of business processes on the whole, and connecting various processes together into one architectural model, while also describing key process attributes and relationships. Though both activities help to create a graphical representation that ultimately serves to improve business processes, modeling incorporates business and economic rules, and is much more than connected activities on a page.

Process models include visual indicators that communicate relationships to other aspects of the enterprise, such as how work products are input and output from processes and activities, what activities are manual and what activities are automated, how processes are supported by human or system resources such as applications or data, and if there are controls or measurements in place. They allow employees and analysts to go deeper into the relationships among processes, subprocesses, and activities and help test and assess any potential outcomes from improvements or changes. Ultimately, process modeling depicts much more information about processes and their hierarchy and structure compared to traditional mapping, and can be used for impact analysis, testing, or simulation.

Modeling benefits include

- Viewing processes and their various relationships from multiple perspectives
- Discovering causes and effects

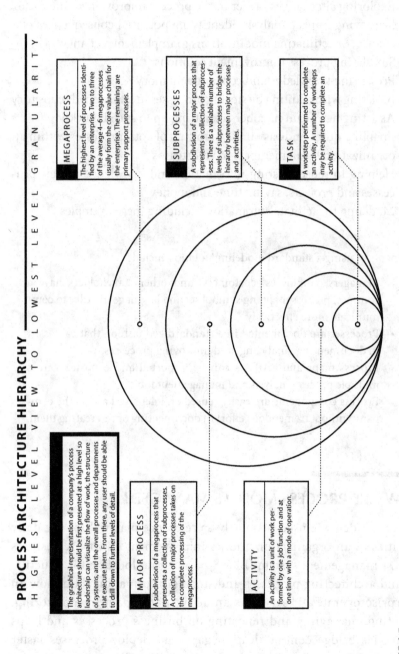

PROCESS ARCHITECTURE HIERARCHY
HIGHEST LEVEL VIEW TO LOWEST LEVEL GRANULARITY

The graphical representation of a company's process architecture should be first presented at a high level so leadership can visualize the flow of work, the structure of systems, and the overall processes and departments that execute them. From there, any user should be able to drill down to further levels of detail.

MEGAPROCESS

The highest level of processes identified by an enterprise. Two to three of the average 4–6 megaprocesses usually form the core value chain for the enterprise. The remaining are primary support processes.

MAJOR PROCESS

A subdivision of a megaprocess that represents a collection of subprocesses. A collection of major processes takes on the complete processing of the megaprocess.

SUBPROCESSES

A subdivision of a major process that represents a collection of subprocesses. There is a variable number of levels of subprocesses to bridge the hierarchy between major processes and activities.

ACTIVITY

An activity is a unit of work performed by one job function and at one time with a mode of operation.

TASK

A workstep performed to complete an activity. A number of worksteps may be required to complete an activity.

FIGURE 4.5
Process architecture hierarchy.

- Improving process understanding through visual analysis
- Discovering errors earlier and reducing system defects
- Exploring alternatives earlier in the process improvement life cycle
- Improving impact analysis, identifying potential consequences of a change, or estimating modifications to implement a change
- Simulating process improvement solutions
- Preserving knowledge and corporate memory
- Assisting with auditing by storing processes in a versioned repository
- Assisting new team members in getting up to speed quickly
- Enabling quick and easy understanding of your processes within an organization by all members of your teams
- Helping to reuse existing information and knowledge in new processes and projects, saving time and money
- Modeling to facilitate automation including these examples

Benefits of using a standard modeling notation include

- Managers, employees, customers, and other stakeholders have a common process mapping symbol set and language in order to communicate more effectively.
- Processes are documented in a standardized fashion that can assist in documenting, analyzing, and improving processes.
- Process maps and artifacts can be imported and exported across multiple process analysis and management tools.
- Process components are easily reused and deployed across the company without tremendous effort in documenting or re-creating them.

HOW ARE PROCESS MODELS MANAGED?

Process models are used primarily as reference material for the daily activities of an organization and its improvement efforts. A business process management system (BPMS) is a central location for structuring and architecting processes and storing information about how an enterprise operates. It serves as an active participant in monitoring, executing, managing, and reporting on business processes and helps companies bridge communication gaps and deploy processes faster with easy-to-use process modeling capability. These tools support the most widely used process modeling styles and notations, as well as mapping types, from basic process maps, flowcharts, and cross-functional swim lane diagrams to powerful standards like BPMN or specialty modeling methods like IDEF0 (Integrated Computer-Aided Manufacturing Definition for Function Modeling). They also provide the ability to fully describe business processes through their connection to other vital aspects of the enterprise (e.g., strategies, master data elements, and performance metrics at various levels of your architecture). BPM tools can also help employees easily create process models using an intuitive interface that automatically manages many of the mapping or drawing tasks. Time-savers like placing shapes quickly, reusing model objects in diagrams, and dragging and dropping sub-processes help capture processes quickly, all while ensuring consistency and standardization.

Administration of a BPM tool includes activities such as creating, storing, managing, and changing process models inclusive of relationships, objects, metadata, business rules, performance measures, and various other components for an enterprise. It includes creating the repository structure or process architecture; defining and maintaining governance procedures to ensure changes are validated, controlled, and approved; mapping processes to systems, data, or any organizational attribute you feel is appropriate; and providing the required infrastructure to enable effective and consistent use of the models in the repository.

Administration of a BPM suite also involves ensuring

- Adequate steps are taken to protect the integrity and security of the repository
- The repository performs at an optimal level and is usable by stakeholders
- Access to the repository is controlled and meets defined availability requirements
- Standards meet the needs of the organization and are adhered to

A business process repository provides a central reference location to ensure consistent communication about how many processes exist, what each process is, how they should be executed, who is responsible for their successful execution, and a clear understanding of the inputs, triggers, and expected results upon process completion. It maintains information needed to adequately define, measure, analyze, improve, and control business processes and helps to promote and support collaboration across functional business units by enabling and enforcing a methodology that focuses on end-to-end process improvement.

Since process models also store information about the individual components used by the various processes, these components can be reused throughout the macroarchitecture, providing scalability and simplifying maintenance. Consistent use of common components avoids redundancy and contradictory information about a business process, as the components only exist once in the repository, but can be visually represented in multiple places while keeping track of these relationships automatically. This allows the impact of a change to a component to be immediately visible wherever it has been used.

A centralized BPM tool also provides a blueprint to manage and control how process changes are introduced and implemented in the enterprise by acting as the system of record for information on process ownership, business rules and controls, technology enablers, subprocesses, and financial information. It may serve primarily as a home for documentation about your company's business processes, or it may be used to simulate various scenarios to evaluate changes, assist with problem solving, and identify and validate the solutions. Today there are a large number of products available for modeling and storing business processes, and we are starting to see more that also have rapid application and process automation capabilities built in. Some vendors who provide tools to this market are outlined in Figure 4.6.

With great power also comes great responsibility. As such, a formal change control procedure needs to be in place and adhered to to protect the accuracy of the various process models within your process architecture. This procedure includes how to request changes, approvals required, timelines, and conflict resolution. When any component is being altered, proper review against the larger ecosystem should be conducted.

The use and administration of a business process repository is a critical component of managing business processes that should be taken as seriously as the administration of any other company asset. As the central blueprint for process management within the organization, it provides a common frame of reference and acts as a method of consistent communication, but it is also the system of record for information on business rules and policies, process ownership, technology relationships, security controls, and financial information and business metrics. Effective and

PROCESS IMPROVEMENT TOOLS _____
V A R I O U S   S U I T E S

FIGURE 4.6
Various process improvement tools.

consistent administration is critical to developing and maintaining the holistic nature of the enterprise's processes through promotion and acceptance of their cross-functional nature.

 Process architecture must be sufficiently rich and capture a reasonably complete set of information about a company's processes, subprocesses, and process elements, along with the relationships, interfaces, and dependencies that exist between them.

WHERE DO I START?

People who are contemplating jumping into a robust process improvement journey and architecting their processes accordingly are often overwhelmed with the task. That's completely normal. After all, architecting a business is not something that you necessarily do every day. To get your journey off to a good start, try these simple confusion-cutting steps:

1. *Identify the purpose of your architecture*: You can begin by defining the purpose of your architecture by asking the following questions:
   - What information is important for the architecture?
   - How much detail is needed to support analysis and decision making?
   - Who will produce or use the architecture?
   - What is the expected return on investment (ROI) or benefit of the architecture?
   - What are the maintenance considerations?

   If you cannot answer these questions, your journey to architect your business processes will likely be difficult. Without a defined purpose, you can waste months mapping and modeling business process diagrams that no one is interested in. By knowing the purpose of your architecture, you can scope the necessary processes and information that are needed to ensure people use your architecture for analysis, improvement, and decision making.

2. *Standardize the models within your architecture*: From the beginning, ensure that processes are standardized in form, structure, and content. Even if the standard changes over time, processes will be fixable in the same way and therefore easier to maintain.

3. *Collect often and catalogue early*: Even before your process architecture model can be used, be sure to collect and catalogue processes and process artifacts as they are created, even in other business units. This will ensure a shared process model across all areas will be created.

4. *Be consistent*: Define the features of your process architecture early and develop processes and assets that match those criteria.

5. *Ensure enterprise awareness and understanding*: In many situations, companies do not think with an enterprise perspective in mind,

where any single change to one process element is likely to have an effect on one or more other process elements. Processes are often intertwined, and changes to any single component must be considered in the context of impact on the others; otherwise, it is easy to fall victim to the law of unintended consequences.

6. *Ensure stakeholders receive consistent messaging and service*: Ensure that mapping interviews and initial discussions are done in a consistent manner. Try to follow a simple framework for information gathering, process design, and administration.

7. *Assist early adopters*: Early adopters are your biggest allies, so be sure to provide proper training and assistance. Work with them to define sensible pragmatic standards and help them create and manage the processes they need.

8. *Have a strategy for legacy artifacts*: Once modeling and architecture standards are defined and processes are being collected, begin to define the strategy for converting old process maps and artifacts to the new process architecture.

9. *Buy a robust BPMS*: Ensure you have a proper BPM tool in place so that modeling activities are simplified, and that your architecture is managed through robust frameworks instead of manually in a document repository.

10. *Ensure proper governance exists*: Once processes are being modeled and structured, ensuring changes and maintenance are done thoughtfully is critical. The following questions are ones that many organizations should ask themselves as changes are needed or proposed:

    - What is the impact of retiring a process?
    - What is the impact of creating a new process?
    - What applications are needed to support a business process?
    - What data does this process use, and are there any master data elements that require attention?
    - What is the impact of replacing or retiring applications or systems?
    - What processes need to be developed to support a new strategy?
    - What policies are related to the various processes?
    - Where are the gaps or redundancies in our application or process portfolio?

    Your answers to these questions often drive the content and maintenance of your architecture. If most questions concern your

PROCESS MODEL
V A R I O U S   V I E W P O N T S

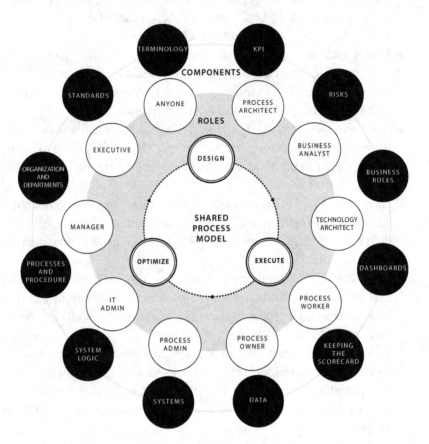

FIGURE 4.7
Shared process model. KPI, key performance indicator.

application portfolio, then focus on defining the application-related processes. If you need to understand how your processes support a new strategy, then focus on the business area in question. Once the major pain points or areas are covered, you can begin to expand the scope of your architecture with new business areas and domains. Ultimately, a capable process architecture combines all processes, business functions, roles, rules, data, and any related enterprise components into a shared process model for all members of an organization to design, execute, and improve processes (Figure 4.7).

CLOSING REMARKS

Business processes represent an organization's key assets. The way a company invents, provides, and controls its core products and services depends on its core business processes. Visualizing these processes is one of the most important factors in understanding them. By modeling your processes in a visual way and structuring them into a unified architecture, you are increasing the potential for success that your organization will understand its processes and have a foundation for analyzing and improving them and effectively communicating change to all that are affected.

With the evolution of process improvement and management and, more recently, taking a comprehensive approach that addresses the major variables in an organization that influence the quality, quantity, and cost of products and services, having a unified process architecture is essential. To keep pace, organizations must find a way for disparate parts to work together in a symbiotic and efficient relationship. Managing businesses within the scope of a POA that deals with the macrostructure of the organization, along with its microrelationships across all units, lets organizations adapt and compete successfully in today's disruptive markets.

Many organizations fail to recognize the importance of an effective, well-defined process architecture early in their process improvement journey, and a lack of architecture can create significant barriers to the achievement of higher levels of maturity or capability. A result of this perceived lack of importance of process architecture is that organizations often pay too much attention to individual and discrete improvements that do not necessarily solve the root cause of issues or even create new issues elsewhere in the organization. A business with a process improvement culture is constantly evolving its capabilities around innovation and working cooperatively and competitively to support new products, satisfy customer needs, and eventually incorporate the next round of innovation and success. Process architecture helps do this in a structured and disciplined manner.

5

Tools for Improving Processes

Problems are at the center of what many people do at work every day. Whether you're solving a problem for a client, supporting those who are solving problems, or discovering new problems to solve, the problems you face can be large or small, simple or complex, easy or difficult. A fundamental part of every employee's job is finding ways to solve those problems. Much of that comes from having a robust improvement toolkit to use when approaching a problem.

Using established tools and techniques will help you improve your approach to gathering information and solving the problems that you and your organization face as you execute business processes. The effective use of these tools and techniques requires their application by the people who actually work on processes, and their commitment to this will only be possible if they are assured that the organization cares about improving quality. Companies must show they are committed by providing the training and implementation support necessary to solve problems in a meaningful way. Once this is known, employees will be more successful at solving problems and, because of this, more successful at what they do. What's more, the organization will begin to build a reputation as one that can handle tough situations in a sensible and positive way, while evolving and improving their operations accordingly. This chapter serves to provide a toolkit intended to provide the practical information you'll need to initiate and successfully carry out process improvement and problem-solving activities in your day-to-day work life.

By the end of this chapter, you should be able to

- Define the meaning of problem solving
- Outline the various stages of problem solving
- Describe several basic tools for process improvement and problem solving

- Outline several advanced tools for process management and problem solving

WHAT IS PROBLEM SOLVING?

Problem solving is the act of defining a problem; determining the cause of the problem; identifying, prioritizing, and selecting alternatives for a solution; and implementing a solution. Good problem-solving skills are fundamentally important if you're going to be successful in your role and in process execution. That's why, when faced with problems, most individuals try to eliminate them as quickly as possible. But have you ever chosen the easiest or most obvious solution, and then realized that you have entirely missed a much better solution? Or have you found yourself fixing just the symptoms of a problem, only for the situation to get much worse? To be an effective problem solver, you need to be systematic and logical in your approach. The following model can help guide you as you assess various problems, design solutions, or improve your current approach to working. By following a structured model, you'll make better overall decisions. And as you increase your confidence with solving problems, you'll be less likely to rush to the first solution, which may not necessarily be the best one.

Problem solving is the act of defining a problem; determining the cause of the problem, and identifying, prioritizing, selecting alternatives for and implementing a solution.

There are several stages to solving a problem:

1. Evaluating the problem
   - Clarifying the nature of a problem
   - Formulating questions
   - Gathering information systematically
   - Collating and organizing data
   - Condensing and summarizing information
   - Defining the desired objective
2. Managing the problem
   - Using the information gathered effectively
   - Breaking down a problem into smaller, more manageable parts

- Using various tools and techniques, such as brainstorming and the five whys, to consider options
- Analyzing these options in greater depth
- Identifying steps that can be taken to achieve the objective

3. Choosing a solution
- Deciding between the possible options for what action to take
- Deciding on further information to be gathered before taking action
- Deciding on resources (time, funding, staff, etc.) to be allocated to this problem

4. Resolving the problem
- Implementing action
- Providing information to other stakeholders; delegating tasks
- Reviewing progress

5. Examining the results
- Monitoring the outcome of the action taken
- Reviewing the problem and problem-solving process to avoid similar situations in the future

 At any stage of **problem solving**, it may be necessary to return to an earlier stage if further problems arise or if a solution does not appear to be working as desired.

BASIC TOOLS FOR PROCESS IMPROVEMENT

As is true in any company, you are likely to be involved with a wide range of activities and processes. At times during these processes and activities, challenges or problems will arise. Often you are able to resolve these issues quickly; however, sometimes you may experience a significant problem, which you find difficult to solve as quickly or as instinctively as you may under other circumstances. The aim of this section is to assist you in developing the skills you need to become an effective problem solver when facing challenging or difficult situations.

You can problem solve anytime you experience a challenge or have a goal to achieve. You can use the problem-solving stages to look for solutions to concerns connected with your processes or other aspects of work life. You can execute the problem-solving steps by yourself, with a colleague, or as a formal process improvement initiative. Problem solving with others is often very effective because you have access to a wide variety of viewpoints and potential solutions. But even with a structured set of stages, dealing with large amounts of data, complex problems, varying opinions, and even political pressures, other tools and techniques are likely needed to help guide you through the process and bring clarity to the situation. This section is intended to provide a resource for you to utilize in all aspects of problem solving, solution design, and when dealing with challenging situations. For each tool, three major aspects are described:

1. What is the tool?
2. What are its benefits?
3. How is the tool used?

What Is 5S?

5S is a simple tool for organizing a workplace environment in a clean, efficient, and safe manner to enhance productivity and visual management and ensure the introduction of standardized working. The five S words are *sort, straighten* (or *set in order*), *shine* (or *scrub*), *standardize* (or *systematize*), and *sustain*. It is a basic methodology for ensuring that operations run smoothly without creating or allowing conditions that create waste. Figure 5.1 describes the 5S model in detail, including its various levels of achievement.

 5S is a simple tool for organizing a workplace environment in a clean, efficient, and safe manner to enhance productivity and visual management and ensure the introduction of standardized working.

What Are Its Benefits?

- The overall workplace becomes cleaner and better organized.
- The manufacturing floor or office operations become safer.
- Visible results enhance the generation of more and better ideas.
- Lead time is reduced.
- Changeover time is reduced by streamlining operations.
- Breakdowns and minor stops are eliminated on production lines.
- Defects are reduced by mistake proofing.
- Clear methods and standards are established.
- In-process inventory is reduced.

5S
L E V E L S   O F   A C H I E V E M E N T

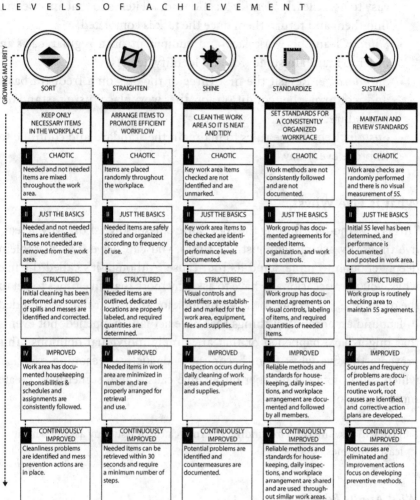

FIGURE 5.1
5S levels of achievement.

- Space usage is improved.
- Customer complaints are reduced.

How Do I Use It?

The 5S steps are as follows:

- *Sort*: Sort out and separate that which is needed and not needed in the area.

- *Straighten*: Arrange items that are needed so that they are ready and easy to use. Clearly identify locations for all items so that anyone can find them and return them once the task is completed.
- *Shine*: Clean the workplace and equipment on a regular basis in order to maintain standards and identify defects.
- *Standardize*: Revisit the first three of the 5S's on a frequent basis and confirm the condition of the workplace using standard procedures.
- *Sustain*: Keep to the rules to maintain the standard and continue to improve every day.

What Is Five Whys?

This is a method for finding the root cause of issues by asking why at least five times. By asking why just five times, you can delve into a problem deeply enough to understand its root cause. Although it's called the five whys, you may occasionally have to ask why more than five times to get to the root cause. Each time you ask why, look for an answer that is grounded in fact and an account of things that have actually happened, not events that might have happened or that are simply individual opinions. This prevents the five whys from becoming a deductive reasoning exercise, which can generate a number of possible causes and, sometimes, create more confusion.

Five whys is a method for finding the root cause of issues by asking why at least five times.

What Are Its Benefits?

- It helps you get to the center of a problem so that it can be addressed at its root cause.
- The activity generally unearths several other problems that are related to the main problem.
- It is easy to use and does not require a great deal of training. Ultimately, it can be used by any person at any level in the organization.
- There is rarely any need to collect data for using this tool, and it also does not call for statistical analysis of any sort.
- If a problem has more than one root cause, then this tool helps to determine the root cause between them.

- It fosters and produces teamwork and teaming within and across the organization.
- It is a guided, team focused exercise. There are no additional costs.

How Do I Use It?

- Assemble a team of people knowledgeable about the area of nonconformance. Include as many personnel as possible.
- On a flip chart, presentation board, or even paper, write out a description of what you know about the problem. Try to document the problem and describe it as completely as possible. Refine the definition with the team. Come to an agreement on the definition of the problem at hand.
- Have the team members ask why the problem as described could occur, and write the answer down underneath the problem description.
- If the answer provided from 3 (above) does not solve the problem, you must repeat steps 3 and 4 until you do.
- If the answer provided seems likely to solve the problem, make sure the team agrees and attempt a resolution using the answer. You may find that there is more than one root cause to the problem.

The **five whys** uses "countermeasures" rather than solutions. A countermeasure is an action or set of actions that seeks to prevent the problem arising again, while a solution just seeks to deal with the situation. As such, countermeasures are more robust, and are more likely to prevent the problem from recurring.

What Is 8D Problem Solving?

Eight disciplines (8Ds) is a problem-solving method developed by the Ford Motor Company and is used to identify, correct, and eliminate recurring problems.

What Are Its Benefits?

- Create a shared understanding about how to systematically solve problems.
- Strengthen cross-functional teamwork, problem solving, and collaboration capabilities.

- Reduce defects, lead times, and costs through effective problem solving.
- Identify the underlying root causes by applying effective problem-solving tools.
- Develop effective process controls to prevent recurrence of known problems.
- Establish a systematic documentation of the problem-solving process.
- Quickly assist the customer with the problem.

How Do I Use It?

- *D0: Prepare for the 8D*
    - Symptom collection
    - Symptom checklist
    - Emergency response action
- *D1: Form a team*
    - Core team structure
    - Team preparation
- *D2: Describe the problem*
    - Problem statement
    - Affinity diagram
    - Is/is not
    - Problem description
- *D3: Interim containment action*
    - Verification of effectiveness
- *D4: Root cause analysis*
    - Differences and changes
    - Root cause theories
    - Verification
    - Process flow diagram
    - Escape point
- *D5: Permanent corrective action*
    - Acceptance criteria
    - Risk assessment
    - Balanced choice
    - Control point improvement
    - Verification of effectiveness
- *D6: Implement and validate*

- Project plan
- Validation of improvements
- *D7*: *Prevention*
  - Similar products and process prevention
  - Systems prevention
  - Standard work or practice
  - Procedures and policy updates
- *D8*: *Closure and team celebration*
  - Documents archived
  - Team lessons learned
  - Before and after comparison
  - Celebrate successful completion

Eight disciplines (8D) problem solving is a method developed by the Ford Motor Company that is used to identify, correct, and eliminate recurring problems.

What Is an Activity Network Diagram?

This is a diagram of project activities that shows the sequential relationships of activities using arrows and nodes. An activity network diagram tool is used extensively in project management and is necessary for the identification of a project's critical path (which is used to determine the expected completion time of the project). Activity network diagrams can also show which steps can be performed in parallel and which must be performed sequentially.

An **activity network diagram** is a diagram of project activities that shows their sequential relationships using arrows and nodes.

What Are Its Benefits?

- Makes dependencies visible between the project activities.
- Organizes large and complex projects, hence allowing a more systematic approach to project planning and scheduling, project execution, and risk management.
- Enables the calculation of the float (slack) of each activity. The float tells you exactly how long an activity can come in late without it impacting the project schedule.

- Encourages the project manager to reduce the project duration by optimizing the critical path and using compression techniques as applicable.
- Increases visibility of impact of schedule revisions, which are usually necessary when major milestones have been missed or when the risk of missing a major milestone looms large.
- Enables the project manager to optimize efficiency by allocating resources appropriately; consequently, the overall cost can be reduced.
- Provides opportunities to respond to the negative risk of going over the schedule by identifying the activities that are most critical.

How Do I Use It?

- Identify the project steps.
- Assign durations, precursors, and gating activities.
- Arrange the steps in a logical pattern that reflects task dependencies.
- Add up the durations of each step in a process.
- The longest duration is the critical path, reflecting the shortest possible time for project completion.

What Is an Affinity Diagram?

This is a method for sorting information, ideas, or items into groups with similar characteristics.

Invented by Kawakita Jiro, affinity diagrams are also known as K-J charts. The idea is to sort ideas into groups with common themes. The method helps to organize large amounts of information into manageable chunks and to make connections between seemingly disconnected ideas more apparent.

An **affinity diagram** is a method for sorting information, ideas, or items into groups with similar characteristics. Invented by Kawakita Jiro, affinity diagrams are also known as K-J charts.

What Are Its Benefits?

- Helps organize ideas that at first seem unrelated
- Makes connections or themes more visible

- Helps prioritize actions and ideas from multiple sources
- Provides visual organization cues
- Helps drive group consensus

How Do I Use It?

- Start by writing every idea on a separate sticky note or index card.
- Lay out all the ideas in random order on a large work service.
- Team members move the notes into groupings that seem logical to them.
- Team members do not speak during the grouping process to avoid intimidating others.
- Any team member can move ideas that someone else has already grouped.
- Not all ideas will fit into a group, so don't worry about loners.
- You can duplicate an idea on a second note or card if it seems to belong in two groups.
- When all team members have completed the sort, speaking is allowed again.
- Discuss patterns and assign themes to each group.

What Is an Attribute Control Chart?

Attribute data are data that can't fit into a continuous scale, but instead are chunked into distinct buckets, like small, medium, or large; pass or fail; and acceptable or not acceptable. This type of control chart evaluates the stability of a process by charting the count of occurrences of a given event in successive samples. The varieties of attribute charts include

- C chart: Counts the number of defects or nonconformities
- P chart: Measures the proportion of defective units
- U chart: Measures defects per unit
- NP chart: Counts the number of defects per sample when the sample size is always the same

Attribute control chart is a type of control chart that evaluates the stability of a process by charting the count of occurrences of a given event in successive samples.

What Are Its Benefits?

- Helps to demonstrate the variability of a process and identify special causes
- Measures the effectiveness of process changes on reducing defects

How Do I Use It?

- If the measured attributes are defects (don't meet one part of acceptance criteria), use an NP or P chart.
- If sample size is constant, use an NP chart.
- If attributes are defectives (don't meet acceptance criteria), use a C chart for a constant sample size or a U chart if not constant.
- Identify upper and lower control limits.
- Plot your counts.

What Is Benchmarking?

This is a process for comparing internal results for a specific metric, such as cost, quality, or time, to the achievements of industry leaders for the purpose of improving the organization's own performance. Benchmarking can measure products, services, or processes against those of organizations known to be leaders in one or more aspects of their operations and provides the necessary insights to help you understand how your organization compares with similar organizations, even if they are in a different business or have a different group of customers.

Benchmarking is a process for comparing internal results for a specific metric, such as cost, quality, or time, to the achievements of industry leaders for the purpose of improving the organization's own performance.

What Are Its Benefits?

- Helps gain an independent perspective about how well they perform compared to other companies
- Clearly identifies specific areas of improvement or opportunity
- Helps validate assumptions
- Prioritizes improvement opportunities
- Sets performance expectations
- Helps monitor company performance and manage change
- Helps determine the "gap" between industry leaders and the organization

How Do I Use It?

- Select the process or subject for benchmarking.
- Identify processes, products, or other performance areas for comparison.
- Choose companies or areas to benchmark.
- Analyze and compare the data and identify opportunities for improvement.
- Adapt and implement the best practices, setting reasonable goals and ensuring company-wide acceptance.
- Implement changes.

What Is Brainstorming?

Brainstorming is a method for problem solving by gathering ideas from a group in which the team generates as many ideas for potential solutions as possible in a defined period of time and in an orderly fashion. The key ingredient is to provide an environment free of criticism for creative and unrestricted exploration of options or solutions. Brainstorming can be used for numerous items, including

- Identifying problem areas
- Identifying areas for improvement
- Designing solutions to problems
- Developing action plans

Brainstorming is a method for problem solving by gathering ideas from a group in which the team generates as many ideas for potential solutions as possible in a defined period of time and in an orderly fashion presents them to the rest of the team.

What Are Its Benefits?

- Often generates very creative solutions.
- Develops large numbers of potential solution ideas in a short period of time.
- Is conducive to teamwork.
- Eliminates unhealthy group behavior.
- Increases participation by all team members, taking advantage of diverse viewpoints and backgrounds.

- Equalizes involvement by all team members.
- Fosters a sense of ownership. Having all members actively participate in the brainstorming process fosters a sense of ownership in the topic discussed.

How Do I Use It?

- Select and prep a team.
- Decide on the method for recording ideas.
- Define the rules (e.g., no judgment or comments on ideas).
- Set a time limit.
- Guide the discussions to keep the group focused, but don't direct the conversation.

 To get the most out of your individual brainstorming session, choose a comfortable place to sit and think. Minimize distractions so that you can focus on the problem at hand.

What Is a Check Sheet?

A check sheet is a form or method for collecting data in real time at the source. Check sheets, or recording tables, are matrices designed to assist in the tallying, recording, and analysis of test results or event occurrences. Check sheets may capture quantitative or qualitative data, and typically consist of check marks on a simple tally sheet. They usually include information on the 5Ws (who, what, when, where, and why).

What Are Its Benefits?

- Quantifies defects by type, cause, or location
- Keeps track of the steps in a process
- Visualizes the probability distribution of a process
- Saves time by showing the frequency distribution as the data are collected

How Do I Use It?

- Construct a grid that includes space for recording measurements and the upper and lower limits for a process.

- The observer places a check in the corresponding box on the grid after each observation.
- At the conclusion of the observation period, examine and assess the shape of the distribution.

What Is a Control Chart?

Control charts are used to indicate whether a process is in control or not and to help determine the cause of the variation. Usually control charts are used for time-series data, but they may also work well for other situations, such as comparisons. If the process is in control, 99.7% of all the measurements will fall inside the upper and lower control limits. Process performance is plotted over time against upper and lower control limits; this helps you readily identify process variations and enables determination of special cause and common cause variations. Figure 5.2 provides a sample control chart.

 A control chart is used to indicate whether a process is in control and to help determine the cause of the variation.

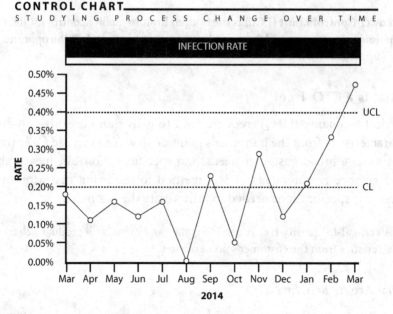

FIGURE 5.2

Control chart. UCL, upper control limit; CL, control limit.

What Are Its Benefits?

- Provides a quick assessment of process stability
- Quickly detects changes in process or instances where a process cannot meet specifications

How Do I Use It?

- Works best for detecting large changes in process variation when using numeric data.
- Create the chart with upper and lower limits, as well as a mean or centerline.
- Plot the data.
- If more than a small number of data points fall outside the upper or lower limits, the process is out of control or not capable of meeting required specifications.

 Upper-Control Limit (UCL) is a value that indicates the highest level of quality acceptable for a product or service. The upper control limit is used in conjunction with the lower control limit to create the range of variability for quality specifications, enabling those within the organization to provide an optimal level of excellence by adhering to the established guidelines.

 Lower Control Limit (LCL) is the bottom limit in quality control for data points below the control (average) line in a control chart. It is the opposite of upper control limit.

What Is a CTQ Tree?

Critical-to-quality (CTQ) trees are used to gather and organize product characteristics from the customer's point of view. You can use CTQ trees to translate broad customer needs into specific, actionable, measurable performance requirements. It is a method for ensuring that a product meets the specifications needed to fully satisfy the customer.

 A **critical-to-quality tree** is used to gather and organize a product's characteristics from the customer's point of view.

What Are Its Benefits?

- It helps to align original product design or new feature ideas to customer requirements.

- It helps in transforming unspecific customer requirements into precise requirements.
- It aids teams in detailing product or process specifications.
- It gives assurance that all the characteristics of the requirements will be fulfilled.

How Do I Use It?

- Start with a conversation with customers or market research to identify the critical needs of your customer base using priority.
- Then, for each need, identify the quality drivers that have to be in place to meet those needs.
- Quantify requirements and assign measurable values.
- Confirm the requirements with customers.
- Analyze the requirements against company goals such as margin or price.
- Generate a detailed project plan that incorporates the steps or tasks to meet the customer's specified needs.

Do a CTQ tree for every need that you identify. You'll then have a comprehensive list of all of the performance requirements that will help you deliver a high-quality product.

What Is Design of Experiments?

This is a set of formal, planned experiments to uncover the effects of process change. It gathers information about process variation by introducing controlled changes or variables and measuring results after each change.

Design of experiments are formal, planned experiments to uncover the effects of process change.

What Are Its Benefits?

- Easy to measure the value of process changes
- Compares treatments or processes against a control sample
- Excellent choice for physical and social sciences or services

How Do I Use It?

- For design of experiments to be effective, the process must be stable and repeatable, so use other techniques to stabilize the process first.
- Establish baseline metrics.
- Introduce a single process change and observe the results.

What Is a Dot Plot?

A dot plot is a simple chart showing data points on a relatively simple scale. Dot plots use simple circles showing the occurrences of variables or values. They are most useful for small data sets of continuous, quantitative data. Figure 5.3 depicts a dot plot.

Dot plot is a simple chart showing data points on a relatively simple scale.

What Are Its Benefits?

- Easy to read and interpret

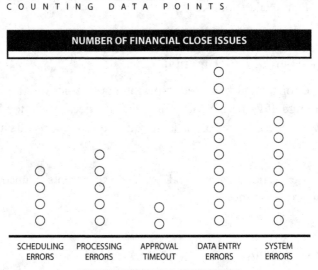

FIGURE 5.3
Dot plot.

How Do I Use It?

- Identify the minimum and maximum value of the data set to determine the scale.
- Place a dot for each item in the data set.

What Is Error Proofing?

This is the process of building safeguards into processes that reduce the possibility of mistakes or defects. It consists of process analysis and design to eliminate or reduce the possibility of mistakes. Error proofing may include tools, jigs, color coding, new equipment, lights, buzzers, design changes, or other safeguards that reduce the likelihood of errors.

Error proofing is a process of building safeguards into processes that reduce the possibility of mistakes or defects.

What Are Its Benefits?

- Reduces defects, saving resources and reducing costs and rework
- Improves customer satisfaction
- Increases teamwork and morale

How Do I Use It?

- Analyze errors or defects occurring in the process.
- Assemble a team to brainstorm potential solutions.
- Prioritize the ideas.
- Implement process changes.

What Is a Fishbone Diagram?

Ishikawa, fishbone, or cause-and-effect diagrams visually represent the causes of a problem—or effect—and help you determine the ultimate source of the problem—the root cause. (This tool is called a fishbone diagram because of its appearance; Ishikawa was its inventor.) The cause-and-effect diagram is used at the beginning of root cause analysis to organize the causes of a problem into categories (people, methods, equipment, materials, measurement, and environment) and prioritize them. Ultimately, it helps identify the potential factors that cause defects or events. Figure 5.4 depicts a fishbone diagram.

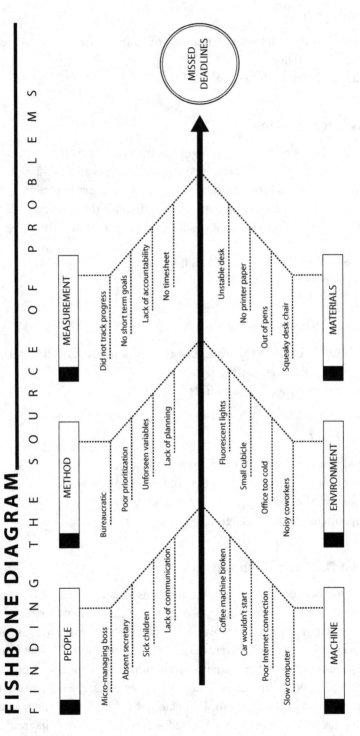

FIGURE 5.4
Fishbone diagram.

A **fishbone diagram** visually represents the causes of a problem (or effect) and help determine the ultimate source of the problem—the root cause. They are also called Ishikawa and cause-and-effect diagrams.

What Are Its Benefits?

- Easy to identify process variation causes
- Helps teams to think about a problem in new ways

How Do I Use It?

- Identify and agree on the problem statement, and write it inside a box on a whiteboard.
- Draw a horizontal arrow line through the box.
- Identify the major categories of potential problems, such as the causes listed above. Write each category as branches off the main arrow line.
- Brainstorm ideas, and write each one on a branching line under the primary causes.
- Use the five whys or another technique to ensure you have identified root causes.

What Is a Flowchart?

Flowcharts visually represent relationships among the activities and tasks that make up a process. They are typically used at the beginning of a process improvement event where you describe process activities, timing, and frequencies. At high levels, flowcharts help you understand process complexity. At lower levels, they can help you analyze and improve the process.

A **flowchart** visually represents relationships among the activities and tasks that make up a process.

What Are Its Benefits?

- Helps visualize a process
- Identifies decision points
- Provides process documentation

- An excellent training aid
- Helps identify unnecessary steps

How Do I Use It?

- Decide on the set of symbols to identify steps, reports, decisions, or other nodes.
- List all process steps in order and assign the designated symbol.
- Place the steps in order, showing the flow of material or data. Add decision points, go/no-go points and branches as necessary to map out the process.

What Is Force Field Analysis?

This is a framework for decisions that identifies forces driving toward an outcome or goal or forces that are blocking or driving away from the outcome. These factors are usually characterized as helping forces and hindering or restraining forces, usually shown exerting pressure on opposite sides of the goal in force field diagrams.

Force field analysis is a framework for decisions that identifies forces driving toward an outcome or goal or forces that are blocking or driving away from the outcome.

What Are Its Benefits?

- Identifies factors that may be preventing goal attainment
- Presents alternative paths to the goal by strengthening positive forces or weakening restraining forces
- Helps identify factors that will move away from equilibrium
- Clarifies the alternative approaches

How Do I Use It?

- Define the change you want to see. Write down the goal or vision of a future desired state. Or you might prefer to understand the present status quo or equilibrium.
- Brainstorm or mind map the driving forces–those that are favorable to change. Record these on a force field diagram.

- Brainstorm or mind map the restraining forces—those that are unfavorable to or opposed to change. Record these on the force field diagram.
- Evaluate the driving and restraining forces. You can do this by rating each force, from 1 (weak) to 5 (strong), and total each side. Or you can leave the numbers out completely and focus holistically on the impact each has.
- Review the forces. Decide which of the forces have some flexibility for change or which can be influenced.
- Strategize. Create a strategy to strengthen the driving forces or weaken the restraining forces, or both. If you've rated each force, how can you raise the scores of the driving forces or lower the scores of the restraining forces, or both?
- Prioritize action steps. What action steps can you take that will achieve the greatest impact? Identify the resources you will need and decide how to implement the action steps. *Hint*: Sometimes it's easier to reduce the impact of restraining forces than it is to strengthen driving forces.

While force field analysis helps you understand the impact of different factors on your decision or change, it can be quite subjective. If you're making an important decision, use it alongside other decision-making tools.

What Is a Histogram Chart?

Histograms charts consist of vertical bars, side by side, that depict frequency distributions within tables of numbers and can help you understand data relationships over time (e.g., the familiar bell curve). Histograms are generally used during process improvement analysis. Histograms are best used to show the frequency of values in continuous data. Usually the independent variable is on the x axis (horizontal) and the dependent variable is on the y axis (vertical), although the axes can also be set up with the opposite positioning. The data are shown as rectangles or blocks. Many people confuse histograms with bar graphs. Although they look similar, histograms represent continuous data and bar graphs represent categories. Usually, the bars in a bar graph are separated, while in histograms they are contiguous.

A **histogram chart** consists of vertical bars, side by side, that depict frequency distributions within tables of numbers and can help you understand data relationships over time (e.g., the familiar bell curve).

What Are Its Benefits?

- Easy to read
- Shows the shape of the distribution of data

How Do I Use It?

- Identify and label the x and y axes on the table and determine the relevant data intervals.
- Plot the occurrences of the data onto the chart.
- Draw boxes around the data points reaching from the x axis to the highest point.

What Is an Interrelationship Diagram?

An interrelationship diagram (ID) shows how different issues are related to one another. It helps identify which issues are causing problems and which are an outcome of other actions. It also shows the strength of each influence. An ID consists of a set of boxes, one representing each issue to be considered. It is organized in a radial pattern on the page. Connecting lines between the boxes indicates their relationship. Arrows show direct relationships and distinguish causes from effects. IDs can be extremely useful when trying to sort out possible causes of a specific problem. Although they do not identify detailed reasons for the problem, they do allow one to analyze broader issues as causes and effects of one another. An ID also works as a planning tool by identifying the interdependence of different elements and suggesting which of the elements may have greater significance.

An **interrelationship diagram** shows how different issues are related to one another. It helps identify which issues are causing problems and which are an outcome of other actions. It also shows the strength of each influence.

What Are Its Benefits?

- Helps identify cause and effect
- Identifies causes with greatest effects
- Shows relationships between issues

How Do I Use It?

- Write a statement defining the issue that the relations diagram will explore. Write it on a card or sticky note and place it at the top of the work surface.
- Brainstorm ideas about the issue and write them on cards or notes. If another tool has preceded this one, take the ideas from the affinity diagram, the most detailed row of the tree diagram, or the final branches on the fishbone diagram. You may want to use these ideas as starting points and brainstorm additional ideas.
- Place one idea at a time on the work surface and ask, "Is this idea related to any others?" Place ideas that are related near the first. Leave space between cards to allow for drawing arrows later. Repeat until all cards are on the work surface.
- For each idea ask, "Does this idea cause or influence any other idea?" Draw arrows from each idea to the ones it causes or influences. Repeat the question for every idea.
- Analyze the diagram:
  - Count the arrows in and out for each idea. Write the counts at the bottom of each box. The ones with the most arrows are the key ideas.
  - Note which ideas have primarily outgoing (from) arrows. These are basic causes.
  - Note which ideas have primarily incoming (to) arrows. These are final effects that also may be critical to address.

What Is an Is/Is Not Matrix?

The is/is not matrix is a tool that helps to precisely identify a problem by organizing known data and ideas about the problem into a table. It identifies where to start looking for causes by isolating the who, what, where, and when about the problem in question. This allows you to narrow your investigation to factors that have an impact and eliminate factors that do not have an impact. The is/is not matrix can be used when

- You're looking for causes of a problem or situation
- You're attempting to isolate factors that affect the problem from those factors that do not

- You're looking for a pattern in the circumstances surrounding a specific situation
- You're trying to identify a problem accurately by organizing available knowledge and ideas about the problem

Is/is not is a matrix that helps to precisely identify a problem by organizing known data and ideas about the problem into a table.

What Are Its Benefits?

- Can be used at any stage of a process improvement effort
- Is a useful tool for problem discovery and resolution
- Offers an exhaustive process for accurate problem definition
- Quickly eliminates factors that cannot be the cause of an issue
- Helps to focus thinking and ensures that action is addressing the problem at hand
- Helps organize information into a structured format

How Do I Use It?

- Describe the problem in the upper left-hand corner. Use general terms so that everyone clearly understands the problem.
- Use the "is" column of the matrix to describe what did or did not occur.
- Determine what objects are affected and what exactly occurs.
- Determine where the problem occurs. This can be a geographic location, a physical location, or on an object.
- Determine when the problem occurs. When did it happen first? When since? What patterns of occurrence have you noticed?
- Determine the extent of the problem. How many objects or occurrences have problems? How many problems? How serious are they?
- Determine who is involved in the problem.
- Use the "is not" column of the matrix to isolate the circumstances that could occur but did not.
- Study the "is" and "is not" columns to identify what is different or unusual about the situations where the problem is, compared to where it is not. What stands out as being odd? Write your thoughts in the column headed "therefore."
- Study the distinctions and look for links to the original problem.

What Is Linear Regression?

This is a regression analysis technique for modeling scalar relationships between a dependent variable and one or more independent variables. It is used to predict or forecast the probable value of unknown variables or to calculate the strength of the relationship between two variables. Predictions are made using a linear equation ($Y = a + bX$). After plotting known data, the strength of the relationship can be gauged by observing the shape of the curve.

Linear regression is a regression analysis technique for modeling scalar relationships between a dependent variable and one or more independent variables.

What Are Its Benefits?

- Provides a basis for extrapolation of future data
- Helps predict outcomes
- Shows trends

How Do I Use It?

- Determine if the relationship between variables is linear, independent, and normally distributed by plotting on a graph.
- Calculate the slope and Y intercept using algebra, Excel, or a statistics application.
- Use the resulting equation to predict future values.

What Is Nominal Group Technique?

This is a more controlled form of brainstorming in which team members write down their ideas for subsequent discussion. It uses no group interaction during the idea generation phase. Each team member writes ideas down independently, and then the group discusses the pros and cons of each idea. It is an excellent technique when some team members are more vocal than others or when some team members think better in silence or are new to the team.

Nominal group technique is a more controlled form of brainstorming in which team members write down their ideas for subsequent discussion.

Each team member writes ideas down independently, and then the group discusses the pros and cons of each idea.

What Are Its Benefits?

- Generates a high number of ideas in a short period of time
- Prevents more assertive team members from hijacking the meeting and forcing their ideas
- Works well with new teams or teams with less vocal members or members who have different native languages

How Do I Use It?

- Identify the problem.
- Set a time limit.
- Each team member writes as many ideas as he or she can think of during the allotted time.
- At the end of the time, the facilitator asks each person for one idea. No discussion of the idea's merits occurs at this point.
- Each idea is written on a board or easel pad so all ideas are visible.
- After each person has given an idea, the facilitator asks each person for another idea. The process continues until there are no more ideas written down.
- Discuss each idea in turn, giving equal weight and time to each idea.

What Is an Organized Process Team?

This team consists of groups of people who work interdependently and cooperatively to meet customer needs or company goals. Teams may be organized by function, department, or cross-functionally to achieve a specific objective. Teams have a common objective and may be part of the formal organization, as in departments, or informal, as in a cross-functional team assigned to a company project or self-organizing to achieve personal objectives or for agile or scrum development cycles.

Organized process team is a group of people who work interdependently and cooperatively to meet customer needs or company goals.

What Are Its Benefits?

- Harnesses the power of multiple viewpoints and experiences for enhanced creativity
- Builds morale and camaraderie, and reduces the monotony of day-to-day jobs
- Builds skills as team members are exposed to new ideas or concepts
- Speeds progress toward goals by distributing tasks

How Do I Use It?

- Build cross-functional teams with members from all groups for projects.
- Select team members to balance personalities, skills, and experience levels, but don't let the highest-ranking member of the team unduly influence the team.
- Use teams of influential people to build acceptance for new ideas or processes.
- Use multilevel teams to build the skill sets of team members.

What Is a Pareto Chart?

The Pareto chart is named after Vilfredo Pareto, who came up with the Pareto principle (or the 80/20 rule), which says that 20% of the factors account for 80% of potential problems. It is a simple technique for prioritizing problem-solving work so that the first piece of work you do resolves the greatest number of problems. It ranks defects, causes, or data from the most significant to the least significant, in descending order. Pareto charts are typically used during process improvement analysis, to understand where to focus improvement for the greatest impact. The left vertical axis of a Pareto chart represents the frequency of occurrence, while the right vertical axis represents the cumulative percentage of the total occurrences.

Pareto chart, named after Vilfredo Pareto, who came up with the Pareto principle (or the 80/20 rule), says that 20% of the factors account for 80% of potential problems.

What Are Its Benefits?

- Breaks big problems into smaller pieces
- Identifies most significant factors
- Shows where to focus efforts
- Allows better use of limited resources
- Highlights importance of specific variations
- Easy to see the impact of variables
- Simplifies deciding on variations or problems to address to meet a specific outcome

How Do I Use It?

- Identify and list problems. Write a list of all of the problems that you need to resolve.
- Identify the root cause of each problem. For each problem, identify its fundamental cause.
- Score each problem.
- Group problems together by root cause.
- Add up the scores for each cause group. The group with the top score is your highest priority, and the group with the lowest score is your lowest priority.
- Fix the issues. Go after the causes of your problems, dealing with your top-priority problem, or group of problems, first and ensuring gaps are closed off.

 While this approach is great for identifying the most important root cause to deal with, it doesn't take into account the cost of doing so. Where costs are significant, you'll need to determine those changes that are worth implementing.

What Is a Paynter Chart?

This is a chart that adds subgroupings to a Pareto chart to represent the run rate or frequency of specific variables. Invented at the Ford Motor Company, it adds the best qualities of a run chart and a Pareto chart to simplify visualization of data impact. The chart groups occurrences by frequency, time, or another characteristic. Paynter charts help by analyzing total cost savings per defect type, for example. Figure 5.5 illustrates a Paynter chart.

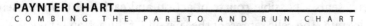

PAYNTER CHART
COMBINING THE PARETO AND RUN CHART

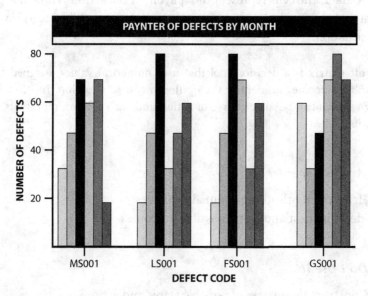

FIGURE 5.5
Paynter chart.

A **Paynter chart** is a chart that adds subgroupings to a Pareto chart to represent the run rate or frequency of specific variables.

What Are Its Benefits?

- Provides insight into variation along multiple dimensions (as in cost and frequency)

How Do I Use It?

- Create Pareto analysis chart based on frequency; group data into subgroups.
- Add a second variable, such as overall cost impact or time.

What Is a Payoff Matrix?

This is a decision tool that uses numerical values assigned to possible outcomes to identify the optimum course of action. It is a table in which each row represents a possible course of action and each column represents a possible state. The cells represent the "payoff" if the action is taken. A payoff matrix helps to clarify the pros and cons of any possible decision in a given situation.

Payoff matrix is a decision tool that uses numerical values assigned to possible outcomes to identify the optimum course of action. In it, each row represents a possible course of action and each column represents a possible state.

What Are Its Benefits?

- Helps clarify thinking about alternatives
- Identifies best and worst possible outcomes

How Do I Use It?

- Construct the matrix of possible states and actions.
- Assign the value of the outcome to each cell.
- Select the alternative that has the most advantageous outcome.

What Is a Prioritization Matrix?

This is a tool to prioritize diverse items into their order of importance by providing a score for each item. It can be especially helpful when there are multiple criteria for importance.

Prioritization matrix is a tool to prioritize diverse items into their order of importance by providing a score for each item.

What Are Its Benefits?

- Clarifies priorities
- Builds consensus

How Do I Use It?

- Identify the objective and assemble the team.
- Brainstorm or use another technique to identify possible actions.

- Identify criteria for judgment.
- Try to ensure the criteria can be expressed objectively, and assign a weighting factor.
- Identify constraints.
- Assign each person on the team a fixed number of points to distribute across actions.
- Multiply the total points by the weighting factor for each item to score.
- List items from highest to lowest score.
- Select the action or actions that will have the most impact.

What Is Process Mapping?

This is a process for creating a visual representation of a process, including who is responsible for each step and how to measure success. It is a tool for the visualization of processes, including details of each step, responsibility, and any instruction or success metrics. It helps to identify non-value-added activities and areas of potential improvement.

Process mapping is step-by-step description of the actions taken by workers as they use a specific set of inputs to produce a defined set of outputs.

What Are Its Benefits?

- Helps ensure that processes align to organizational objectives
- Identifies non-value-added steps
- Helps ensure effective and efficient processes

How Do I Use It?

- Similar to a flowchart, identify the steps in a process and the order in which they are performed.
- Add details for responsibility and external process documentation for specific steps.
- Analyze the process for efficiency, effectivity, and waste.

What Is a Project Selection Checklist?

This checklist highlights elements for consideration when selecting and prioritizing projects. It is a method for scoring, ranking, or prioritizing projects to determine which ones to undertake.

What Are Its Benefits?

- Ranks projects based on consistent, objective criteria
- Identifies and balances risk and reward for competing projects
- Helps build consensus

How Do I Use It?

- Identify key criteria such as cost, return on investment, risk, market potential, or government regulations.
- Decide on a simple weight or ranking criteria.
- Rank projects for each criteria.

What Is a QMS Review?

This is a standardized review of the internal quality management system (QMS). International Organization for Standardization (ISO) certification and many industry standards require periodic reviews. The review process and timetable should be documented to ensure consistency.

 QMS review is a standardized review of an internal quality management system. International Organization for Standardization (ISO) certification and many industry standards require periodic reviews of quality systems and frameworks.

What Are Its Benefits?

- Helps ensure compliance with certifications and industry or government regulations
- Ensures suitability, adequacy, and effectiveness of a quality system

How Do I Use It?

- Define the frequency.
- Identify all inputs and outputs, including customer feedback, conformance data, and corrective actions.
- Identify a cross-functional team that includes at least one top-level manager.
- Assess quality performance and identify areas of noncompliance or poor performance for corrective action.

What Is a Radar Chart?

This is a graphical method for displaying small sets of multivariate data. It is also known as a spider chart, with each of the spokes representing one variable. The value for the variable is plotted and connected to the adjacent variables by a line. The distance along the radius shows the relative strength or commonality of each variable.

> A **radar chart** is a graphical method for displaying small sets of multivariate data. Also known as a spider chart, each of the spokes represents one variable.

What Are Its Benefits?

- Easy to identify outliers or areas of similarity
- Identifies relative strengths and weaknesses of alternatives

How Do I Use It?

- Create a circle with a radius for each variable to plot.
- It may be easier to read the chart if it includes concentric circles at set points inside the outermost ring.
- Plot points on the appropriate radius.
- Connect points.
- If plotting multiple examples on a single chart, use a different color for each; if using separate charts for comparisons, put the charts side by side.

What Is a Responsibility Chart?

Also often known as RACI charts, responsibility charts show participation by role in the activities of a project or process. It uses a matrix or diagram to show these responsibilities for activities in a project or process. Usually, participants will be assigned as responsible, accountable or approver, consulted or informed. Participants in an overall project may also have no responsibility, accountability, influence, or input to a particular step in the project.

> A **responsibility chart (RACI)** is a matrix or diagram that shows responsibilities for activities in a project or process.

What Are Its Benefits?

- Makes roles clear
- Fosters teamwork and accountability
- Ensures communication and collaboration

How Do I Use It?

- List tasks or project steps in the left column.
- List roles across the top row, one role per column.
- Decide on the meaning and responsibility codes to use, since there are many variations besides RACI.
- Assign one of the codes to a role for each task.
- It is usually best to have one and only one role assigned per task or responsibility, although that role may ask others for assistance.

What Is a Run Chart?

This is a graph that displays observed data or variations in a time sequence. It is a simple, graphical representation of observed values in sequence.

 A **run chart** is a graph that displays observed data or variations in a time sequence. it is a simple, graphical representation of observed values in sequence.

What Are Its Benefits?

- Makes it easy to spot anomalies such as outliers or shifts in a process
- Helps identify factors affecting processes
- Simple to produce

How Do I Use It?

- Collect data and plot points on a graph where the y axis represents a variable and the x axis represents time.
- Add a line for median values or plot multiple observations in different colors.

What Is a Scatter Diagram?

Scatter charts display relationships between dependent (predicted) and independent (prediction) variables. They are used during hypothesis testing to determine if there is a correlation between two variables and how strong the correlation is. Less scattering indicates stronger correlation. The graph has different variables on the horizontal and vertical axes. Each data point is positioned on the graph at the intersection point of the two variables plotted on the respective axes. The result is a series of dots that show the distribution of data and the correlation of the variables.

A scatter diagram is a graph with different variables on the horizontal and vertical axes. Each data point is positioned on the graph at the intersection point of the two variables plotted on the respective axes. The result is a series of dots that show the distribution of data and the correlation of the variables.

What Are Its Benefits?

- Helps visualize the effect of changes to a variable
- Shows nonlinear relationships
- Demonstrates correlation and trends

How Do I Use It?

- Plot the control variable on the horizontal axis and the dependent variable on the vertical axis.
- Place a dot for each observation at the corresponding value of the two variables.
- Visualize this as the intersection of two straight lines beginning at the point on the axes, and place the dot at the intersection point.
- Do not actually draw these lines.
- If desired, add a trend line, an identity line, or another set of scatter points from a different related set.

What Is a SIPOC?

A SIPOC is a high-level process map that examines the details of how an organization satisfies a particular customer requirement (Figure 5.6). The process map covers the entire value chain, from supplier to customer, for a particular customer requirement. The name derives from the first letter of the names of items included in the map:

- Supplier: The company that provides the material to be worked on
- Input: The material or information

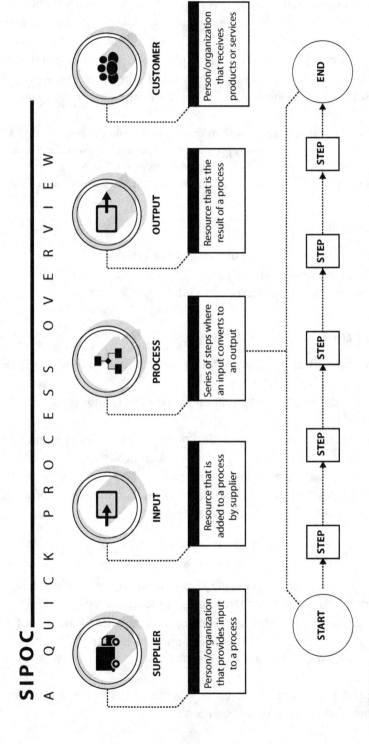

FIGURE 5.6
SIPOC.

- Process: The internal steps
- Output: The product or service delivered to the customer
- Customer: The next step in the process or the final customer

 SIPOC is a high-level process map that examines the details of how an organization satisfies a particular customer requirement or delivers a product or service.

What Are Its Benefits?

- Helps identify areas that require improvement
- Enhances process effectiveness
- Pinpoints waste
- Sharpens focus on customer needs
- Provides a view of cross-functional activities

How Do I Use It?

- Determine the high-level process steps, including the starting and stopping points, and put them in simple noun–verb format.
- Identify the cue to act and the conclusion.
- List all process outputs, customers, inputs, and suppliers in columns.

What Is a Spaghetti Diagram?

A **spaghetti diagram** is a map of the production process from requirement to delivery. It is a complex map of the actual flow of an entire process, including all employee actions. The diagram gets its name from its frequent resemblance to a plate of spaghetti when it has been completed.

 A **spaghetti diagram** is a map of the production process from requirement to delivery. A complex map of the actual flow of an entire process, including all employee actions. The diagram gets its name from its frequent resemblance to a plate of spaghetti when it has been completed.

What Are Its Benefits?

- Identifies the actual process and areas of waste
- Helps brainstorm ideas for improvements

- Shows interdepartmental interactions
- Improves collaboration

How Do I Use It?

- Record the process steps and use arrows to show the flow to the next step.
- Capture exceptions, because they represent opportunity to refine the process.
- Record the time spent on each activity.
- Show material storage, movement, inspection, and holding stops, along with times and responsible roles.
- Create an ideal state diagram and generate projects to move the process from spaghetti to ideal.

What Is a Stakeholder Map?

This chart analyzes and identifies key project influencers, which can help to win support for a project or improve the likelihood of its success by identifying stakeholder motivations.

A **stakeholder map** analyzes and identify key project influencers, which can help to win support for a project or improve the likelihood of its success by identifying stakeholder motivations.

What Are Its Benefits?

- Helps shape projects for success
- May help garner resources and organizational support for the project
- Builds teamwork and consensus

How Do I Use It?

- Identify stakeholders. Stakeholders are any people who may be affected by the project or who have power over its success or the allocation of necessary resources.
- Create a chart with a large square divided into four quadrants.
- Show interest on the horizontal axis and power along the vertical axis.

- Label the upper quadrants "keep satisfied" on the left and "manage closely" on the right.
- Label the lower quadrants "monitor" on the left and "keep informed" on the right.
- Map each identified stakeholder to the appropriate spot on the grid.
- Plan your work and interaction with the stakeholders accordingly.

What Is a Survey?

A survey is a tool used to gather information through polling or a questionnaire. Surveys may be structured or unstructured, and may include a mix of quantitative and qualitative questions, depending on the audience and the desired result.

A **survey** is a tool used to gather information through polling or a questionnaire.

What Are Its Benefits?

- Collects large amounts of data quickly
- Inexpensive and quick to create and administer
- Easily adaptable to a wide range of situations

How Do I Use It?

- Decide on the survey objective and methodology (mail, phone, email, or in-person interviews).
- Construct the questionnaire.
- Have someone review the questionnaire to help eliminate any built-in bias.
- Administer the survey and tally the results.

What Is a SWOT Analysis?

A SWOT analysis chart is typically shown with four quadrants, designed for rapid analysis of a market or competitive situation, accounting for the analysis of organizational strengths, weaknesses, opportunities, and threats (Figure 5.7).

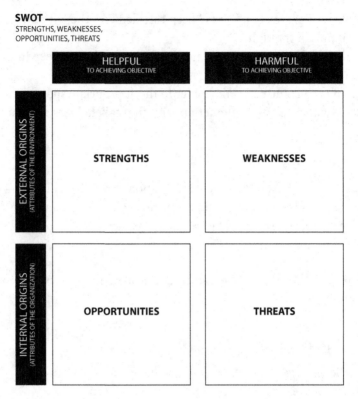

FIGURE 5.7
SWOT chart.

 A **SWOT analysis chart** is typically shown with four quadrants, designed for rapid analysis of a market or competitive situation, accounting for organizational strength, weakness, opportunity, and threat.

What Are Its Benefits?

- Easy to read and concise
- Quick to construct
- Helps in planning to reach objectives

How Do I Use It?

- Identify key internal and external factors that affect the objective.
- Match strengths to opportunities to uncover competitive advantages.
- Convert weaknesses or threats into strengths or opportunities in new markets or positioning.

What Is a Tollgate Review?

This is a checkpoint to verify that all required activities have been completed before moving on to the next phase or project. It is a team review process typically carried out at key points in the project to ensure that activities have been completed as required in the project plan. Tollgate reviews are similar to go/no-go analysis in that they help in the decision to move forward with the next phase of a project or plan.

 Tollgate review is a checkpoint to verify that all required activities have been completed before moving on to the next phase or project.

What Are Its Benefits?

- Helps determine whether all project phase requirements have been met
- Builds consensus and aids in communication

How Do I Use It?

- Gather all project team members.
- Discuss each activity in the project phase to ensure it has been completed.
- Use a checklist to enhance visibility.
- If all activities are successfully completed, move on to the next phase of the project.
- If incomplete or unsatisfactorily completed activities remain, put a plan in place to remedy the defect.

ADVANCED TOOLS FOR PROCESS IMPROVEMENT

Many of the tools defined in the prior section are simple to use and reasonably well known. In fact, some of them are considered essential to quality assurance and process management.

However, advanced process improvement requires some additional, more complex tools or concepts. There are also several more advanced tools you can use to understand and improve processes during a process improvement event. Each tool helps you identify sources of variation and aids in the analysis, documentation, and organization of the information, which leads to process improvement and better problem solving.

What Is DRIVE?

DRIVE is an acronym for an approach to problem solving and process improvement based on five steps. The DRIVE methodology consists of the following steps:

1. Define the scope of the process, deliverables, and success criteria.
2. Review the current process and collect data.
3. Identify improvements and necessary changes.
4. Verify the improvements will meet the defined goals and prioritize changes based on impact.
5. Execute the plan by implementing the changes and measuring results.

DRIVE is an acronym for an approach to problem solving and process improvement based on five steps.

What Are Its Benefits?

- Provides a framework for process improvement and problem solving
- Builds project and improvement consensus
- Helps identify areas for improvement and ensures that the essential elements of measurement, analysis, and feedback are included in the plan

How Do I Use It?

- D—Define: You should define (a) the scope of your problem and (2) the success criteria measurements, including deliverables and success factors that you agree on.
- R—Review: Review the current situation of the problem, understand the background of the problem, and determine and collect information—performance data, problem areas, and improvement options.

- I—Identify (determine): Identify (determine) improvement options or solutions to the problem. What changes do you need to make to improve your process to rectify the problem?
- V—Verify: Verify (check) whether the determined improvement options or solutions will bring those results that we defined as the success criteria measurements.
- E—Execute (implement): Plan and execute improvement options or solutions, and check the results.

In many cases, individuals like to add an R to the acronym (DRIVER) in order for people and teams to reflect (R) on the outcome and revise any actions as necessary.

What Is ICOR?

ICOR stands for inputs, constraints, output, and resources. It is an internationally accepted process analysis methodology for process mapping. It allows processes to be broken down into simple, manageable, and more easily understandable units. The maps define the inputs, outputs, controls, and resources for both the high-level process and the subprocesses.

ICOR stands for inputs, constraints, output, and resources, and is an internationally accepted process analysis methodology for process mapping.

What Are Its Benefits?

- Helps to train people on new processes
- Can be created quickly
- Highly visual

How Do I Use It?

- Start with a box representing the overall process.
- List the inputs on the left, with an arrow drawn toward the box.
- List constraints above the box, with an arrow drawn toward the box.
- List resources below the box, with an arrow drawn toward the box.
- List outputs to the right of the box, with an arrow drawn toward the box.
- Order each list from most to least in terms of impact.

What Is a Problem-Solving Funnel?

This is a method of identifying the root cause of a problem by moving from vague awareness that a problem exists through specific steps that narrow the focus and bring the organization to the root cause and possible solutions. It is a graphic representation of the Toyota problem-solving method. The top of the funnel includes a large or vague problem statement, which the problem-solving team works to clarify. As the team grasps the situation better, they use the five whys to identify the root cause and other techniques to identify possible countermeasures to solve the problem.

A **problem-solving funnel** is a method of identifying the root cause of a problem by moving from vague awareness that a problem exists through specific steps that narrow the focus and bring the organization to the root cause and possible solutions.

What Are Its Benefits?

- Practical and quick
- Forces focus on specific and detailed problem definition
- Drives to root cause

How Do I Use It?

- Identify the problem and assemble the team.
- Work toward clarification of the real situation or problem.
- Measure the current results.
- Use the five whys or another tool to identify the root cause.
- Brainstorm potential countermeasures and solutions.
- Implement highest-impact countermeasure.
- Measure and evaluate results.
- Standardize the new process if warranted.

What Is Statistical Process Control?

Statistical process control (SPC) is a quality control method for monitoring a process to ensure it reaches its full potential for producing conforming products by eliminating or reducing waste, scrap, and rework. It is also a strategy for reducing the variability in deliveries, materials, equipment, and even attitudes, which are the cause of most quality problems. As deviations occur, the team intervenes to prevent creating defective goods. SPC emphasizes early detection of potential issues to prevent problems, rather than correction of problems later in the process. SPC also helps identify whether a process is in control (stable and exhibiting only random variation) or out of control and needing attention.

Statistical process control is a quality control method for monitoring a process to ensure it reaches its full potential for producing conforming products by eliminating or reducing waste, scrap, and rework.

What Are Its Benefits?

- Reduces costs by eliminating scrap, rework, and waste.
- Better resource utilization increases throughput.
- Helps improve customer satisfaction from on-time delivery.

How Do I Use It?

- Establish the process.
- Measure process output.
- Intervene as soon as deviations or trend analysis indicates a problem is developing.
- Resolve the issue.

What Is Statistical Sampling?

This is the use of a representative subset of a population to make inferences about the entire population. It is a method of quality assurance that requires testing representative samples from a batch or lot to ensure the material meets specifications and is suitable for use. Depending on the number or proportion of defects, the entire lot may be accepted, rejected, or in some cases, individually inspected. The number of items to inspect in a sample is calculated based on the lot size and the degree of assurance and accuracy necessary.

Statistical sampling involves using a representative subset of a population to make inferences about the entire population.

What Are Its Benefits?

- Saves time and resources

How Do I Use It?

- Define the population and the acceptable level of risk.
- Calculate the required sample size that will provide the right degree of certainty that the lot is acceptable.
- Randomly select the items to be inspected.
- Perform inspections.
- Calculate the acceptance ratio.
- Disposition the lot as acceptable, rejected, requires rework, or needs further sampling.

What Is Theory of Constraints?

The theory of constraints (TOC) aims to maximize throughput by managing one or more constraining resources that impose limits on the entire process. In any process, total throughput is limited by the capacity of a small number of constrained resources. By designing a process that maximizes the output through the constraints, overall throughput is optimized. It makes no sense to optimize resources that do not constrain throughput, because that merely increases potential idle time. The concept was popularized in the book *The Goal* by Eliyahu Goldratt in 1984. The theory is often paraphrased as "a chain is only as strong as its weakest link."

 Theory of constraints, also known as TOC, is a management method which aims to maximize throughput by managing one or more constraining resources that impose limits on the entire process.

What Are Its Benefits?

- Maximizes total process throughput
- Minimizes inventory investment and costs of process improvements
- Helps prioritize process improvement efforts
- Simplifies planning and scheduling

How Do I Use It?

- Identify the constraints by evaluating the maximum throughput of each resource.
- Decide how to best utilize the constrained resource.
- Subordinate all other steps in the process to this constraint.
- Take steps to improve the capability of the constrained resource.
- When a constraint breakthrough occurs, begin the process again to identify the next constraint.

CLOSING REMARKS

Problem solving is an exceptionally important workplace skill. Everybody can benefit from having good problem-solving skills, as we all encounter problems on a daily basis; some of these problems are more severe or complex than others. Unfortunately, there is no one way in which all problems can be solved, but being a competent and confident problem solver will create many opportunities for you. By using a well-developed problem-solving model and accompanying tools and techniques like the five whys and process mapping, you can approach the process of problem solving systematically, and be comfortable that the decisions you make are both grounded and concrete. All process improvement tools share many common features. They share the philosophy that processes can always be improved. They share the assumption of measurement and control being keys to improvement. And lastly, they share the faith in the power of the workers closest to a process to be able to improve it.

6

Process Improvement Culture

Culture is the invisible bond that ties employees together. The processes, people, values, and structures of an organization ultimately represent its culture. The importance of corporate culture lies in its close association to the ways employees think and operate. Unfortunately, many individuals do not understand their corporate culture, and many don't even acknowledge it exists; yet it is the heart and soul of any enterprise. Things like products, strategies, and even processes can be duplicated. The only truly unique identifier is the set of norms and values that make up an organization and its culture. As such, it is a critical component in any business's ultimate success or failure.

To have an organization that focuses on process improvement, culture must play a starring role, and the organization itself should foster an attitude of continuous improvement. Employees must believe the purpose of the organization is important, enjoy their work and take pride in project outcomes, and also be recognized and appreciated in their efforts to improve. When an organization adopts a culture of process improvement, employees feel empowered and can sustain themselves in pursuing higher-quality targets or making improvements without the need for constant leadership intervention. This chapter serves as an introduction to organizational culture and how to manage and build a culture of success. Understanding these concepts and recognizing the role you play within your organization will provide you with the information needed to shape the performance of your business and help you build your desired culture.

By the end of this chapter, you should be able to

- Define the meaning of culture and how it dictates behavior in organizations
- Understand the meaning of a process improvement culture

- Outline the phases of cultural change
- Explain how to manage cultural change
- Outline leadership's role in process improvement
- Describe how human resources (HR) can assist with transformation initiatives

WHAT IS CULTURE?

Every company has its own unique personality, just like every individual. The unique personality of an organization is referred to as its culture. In organizations today, corporate culture is an invisible, but powerful force that influences the behavior of all members of an organization. Corporate culture is commonly referred to as the shared attitudes, values, principles, and beliefs that characterize a company and define its nature and approach to managing employees, customers, investors, and the greater community. Your company culture defines the way in which it interacts with itself and with the outside world. It's the formula that guides the business, as well as inspires and motivates employees, and is integral toward attracting and attaining great talent and creating a fun, happy, and motivating work environment.

 Culture is the shared attitudes, values, principles and beliefs that characterize a company and define its nature and approach to managing employees, projects, investors, customers, and the greater community.

How the organization chooses to conduct its business, how much freedom there is in decision making, and how information or messages flow throughout the company all matter and are all influenced by culture. To change or influence an organization's culture, one must obtain a holistic perspective of the culture that is present today, and determine the core values that are important to the business and that leadership and employees alike can promote in order to influence this shift. There are three main areas that most commonly impact corporate culture:

1. *Corporate behaviors*: The behaviors of employees and their leadership that are most commonly displayed

2. *Corporate values*: The values employees associate meaning to and continually promote, and drive what is occurring in a company
3. *Corporate structures*: The mechanisms by which a company manages tasks and people

In a healthy culture, employees view themselves as part of a team and gain satisfaction from helping the overall company succeed and improve itself. When employees sense that they are contributing to a successful endeavor, their level of commitment and productivity, and subsequently the quality of the company's products or services, are likely to improve. In contrast, employees in an unhealthy culture tend to view themselves as individuals, distinct from the company, and focus primarily on their own needs. They only perform the most basic requirements of their roles, and their main, and perhaps only, motivation is their compensation.

There are several types of corporate values, both positive and negative, so you will need to choose the ones that are right for you and your organization. Here are some examples of core values from which you may wish to choose or avoid:

Positive values: Customer focus, performance, safety, innovation, service oriented, reliable

Negative values: Money, status, power, control, promoting winning over others

WHAT IS A PROCESS IMPROVEMENT CULTURE?

Organizations cannot improve unless they continually seek out and solve their problems. For many companies, that means undertaking a profound cultural change. When a company consistently engages its people in problem solving as part of their daily work, employees are more motivated and do their jobs better, and the organization's performance improves as a result. Through a combination of process orientation and behavior setting, companies can overwhelmingly encourage the changes they want to see. In this section, we look at four common traits that companies need to develop as part of a conscious effort to build a process improvement culture (Figure 6.1).

PROCESS IMPROVEMENT CULTURE _____
COMMON TRAITS

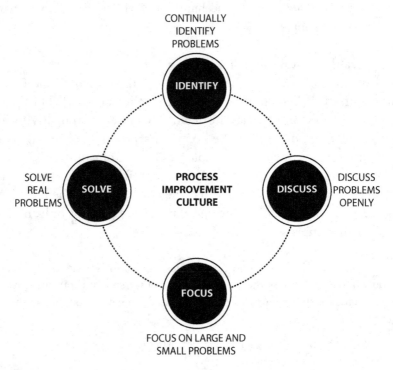

FIGURE 6.1
Common traits of a process improvement culture.

1. *Continually identify problems*: Before a problem can be acknowledged, you have to be aware of it. Identifying problems, particularly before they grow into major issues, is a skill that can be learned. In process improvement, most problems can be attributed to some form of waste or variability. Learning how to spot these factors as they arise is one of the most important skills leaders and their organizations can develop. Organizations can often achieve significant improvements by simply exploring what is preventing them from using best practices consistently across their workforce, or from executing processes without delay or disruption. Once these issues are resolved and stable performance is realized, new gaps are often identified that require exploration.

2. *Discussing problems openly*: Great problem solving begins with the ability to acknowledge problems and a willingness to see them

without judgment. When an organization treats problems as bad things or punishes people for bringing them out into the open, it makes people uncomfortable, resulting in an environment where problems stay hidden and do not get fixed. Some leaders are quick to point fingers, or rush to judgment instead of taking the time needed to truly analyze problems and uncover their root causes. Conversely, some people resort to avoidance strategies, dodging problems to keep the peace with colleagues. These sorts of practices can be hard habits to break, even for those who know how damaging they can be, and neither attributing blame nor brushing a problem under the carpet is helpful. Organizations that embrace process improvement understand that when a problem is properly identified, the root cause usually turns out to be an underlying factor that the organization can address, such as inadequate training, a lack of transparency, poor communication, or misaligned incentives, not a particular group or individual. Raising and analyzing problems is not just normal, but desirable and critical to success in process-focused organizations.

3. *Focusing on large and small problems*: Many organizations today believe that implementing big strategic change or transformation projects is central to changing their organization. However, this opinion misses an important truth: businesses don't rise or fall by big projects alone. Small problems matter and are often more critical to day-to-day operations, and the only way to manage these everyday common issues is to detect and solve them as they arise. This sort of mindset requires an organization to develop a more distributed problem-solving capability where leaders carry the responsibility for developing analytical problem-solving behaviors and ensuring those behaviors are adopted at every level within the company. The ultimate goal is for everyone in the company to take the initiative to solve the problems that are most relevant to them while meeting the institution's growth aspirations.

4. *Solving real problems*: All too often, employees fail to define the root cause of a problem, rely on instinct rather than facts, or jump to conclusions rather than stepping back and asking probative questions. They fall into the trap of confusing decisiveness with problem solving, and therefore rush into action instead of taking the needed time to examine and reflect. Why does this happen so often? Because following a systematic problem-solving process takes discipline and

patience, and there are no shortcuts, even for seasoned leaders who possess a wealth of experience. An organization that consistently uses simple problem-solving approaches across its entire enterprise can achieve more than just greater rigor in asking the right questions; it can create a new shared language that helps people build capabilities more quickly and collaborate across internal boundaries more effectively.

An effective process for identifying and solving problems involves four steps, as outlined in Figure 6.2:

1. *Plan*: Clarify what should be happening and what is happening, learning as much as possible about the problem and identifying its root cause.
2. *Do*: Generate possible solutions and craft the ideal solution that tackles the root cause, eliminating the symptom that the problem causes. Test the solution to ensure it has the expected impact.
3. *Check*: Measure how effective the identified solution is, and gather any learning from it that could make it even better.
4. *Act*: The last step is to incorporate the solution, with training and follow-up to ensure everyone has adopted the new method. This should eliminate any possibility of recurrence.

The plan–do–check–act (PDCA) cycle provides a simple but effective approach for problem solving and allows solutions to be appropriately tested before they are implemented. It can be used in all sorts of environments, including new product development, service delivery, technology projects, operations, finance, and marketing.

An organization with a process-focused culture understands the need for problem solving and continuous improvement. Organizations that are siloed and divide themselves up instead of becoming more collective in nature often find that they struggle in the marketplace. The truly excellent cultures are those that challenge themselves and their own success to understand the behaviors and thinking that have led them to making good decisions.

Creating a culture of process improvement does not happen overnight; however, once you have reached a point of employee engagement, you can build a culture of leaders and employees who truly

PDCA
IDENTIFYING AND SOLVING PROBLEMS

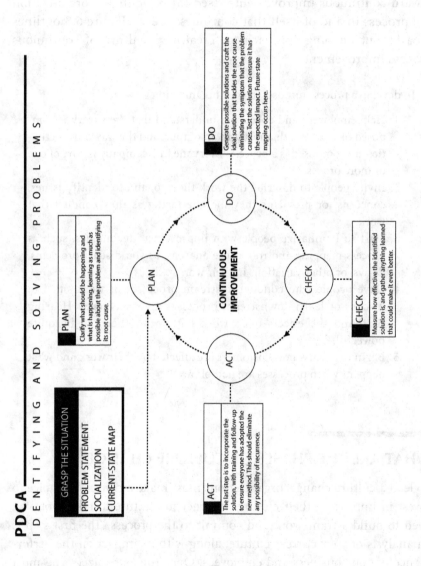

GRASP THE SITUATION

PROBLEM STATEMENT
SOCIALIZATION
CURRENT-STATE MAP

PLAN

Clarify what should be happening and what is happening, learning as much as possible about the problem and identifying its root cause.

DO

Generate possible solutions and craft the ideal solution that tackles the root cause eliminating the symptom that the problem causes. Test the solution to ensure it has the expected impact. Future state mapping occurs here.

CHECK

Measure how effective the identified solution is, and gather anything learned that could make it even better.

ACT

The last step is to incorporate the solution, with training and follow-up to ensure everyone has adopted the new method. This should eliminate any possibility of recurrence.

CONTINUOUS IMPROVEMENT

PLAN   DO   ACT   CHECK

FIGURE 6.2
PDCA—a path to continuous improvement.

believe that improvement is a part of their job. Process improvement culture is not just a philosophy, but a pursuit of purpose, a way of life, and it has powerful effects to improve engagement, take ownership, become more customer focused, and deliver better solutions. Moving toward continuous improvement–based thinking in any organization is a process in and of itself that continues forever. Figure 6.3 outlines a basic, but ongoing approach for creating a culture of continuous process improvement.

To develop a process mindset in your organization

1. Help employees and colleagues understand that their work is composed of activities that result in an output, and the way those activities are composed is a process. Everyone in a company is part of one or more processes.
2. Invite people to describe the work they do, and to identify issues, concerns, or problems they may be facing as they conduct that work.
3. Start to familiarize people with improvement techniques, such as process mapping and root cause analysis, as you discuss problems, delays, or other variations in their work.
4. Have people who conduct upstream processes or work sit in to discuss or learn downstream processes and vice versa. Hearing firsthand the effects one's work has on another can be quite powerful.
5. Begin to discuss how customers are affected by their work and what happens when processes are not followed.

WHAT ARE THE PHASES OF CULTURE CHANGE?

To lead a culture change, organizations must make a conscious choice to invest in improving their culture. In order for culture to take root, you need to build a framework and commit to the process. The first step is an analysis of your current culture, along with its impact on the performance of your business and employees. Once this is realized, you must then identify the values and culture you strive for. Set your goals, and build and implement your plan based on the values, behaviors, and structures. Most importantly, ensure you make conscious efforts in continuous communication throughout all cycles of the process. Studies show that

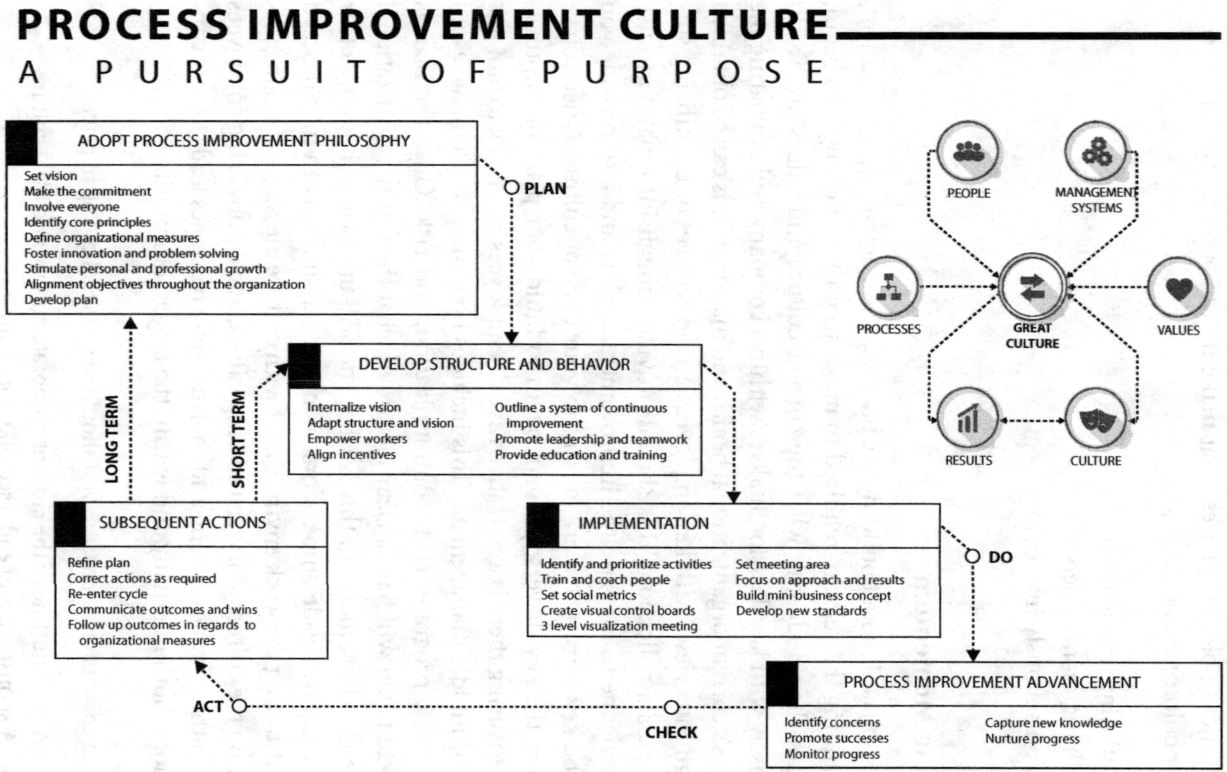

PROCESS IMPROVEMENT CULTURE
A PURSUIT OF PURPOSE

GREAT CULTURE

- MANAGEMENT SYSTEMS
- PEOPLE
- PROCESSES
- VALUES
- CULTURE
- RESULTS

PLAN

ADOPT PROCESS IMPROVEMENT PHILOSOPHY
- Set vision
- Make the commitment
- Involve everyone
- Identify core principles
- Define organizational measures
- Foster innovation and problem solving
- Stimulate personal and professional growth
- Alignment objectives throughout the organization
- Develop plan

DEVELOP STRUCTURE AND BEHAVIOR
- Internalize vision
- Adapt structure and vision
- Empower workers
- Align incentives
- Outline a system of continuous improvement
- Promote leadership and teamwork
- Provide education and training

SHORT TERM

IMPLEMENTATION
- Identify and prioritize activities
- Train and coach people
- Set social metrics
- Create visual control boards
- 3 level visualization meeting
- Set meeting area
- Focus on approach and results
- Build mini business concept
- Develop new standards

DO

PROCESS IMPROVEMENT ADVANCEMENT
- Identify concerns
- Promote successes
- Monitor progress
- Capture new knowledge
- Nurture progress

CHECK

SUBSEQUENT ACTIONS
- Refine plan
- Correct actions as required
- Re-enter cycle
- Communicate outcomes and wins
- Follow up outcomes in regards to organizational measures

LONG TERM

ACT

FIGURE 6.3
Embedding a process improvement philosophy.

for cultural values to be successfully adopted in a business or a community, there must be constant reminders of them everywhere. As originally outlined by Caroline Taylor in her book, *Walking the Talk*, there are three main building blocks (phases) that make up the basic framework necessary for culture to spread:

1. Building momentum
2. Changing mindsets
3. Continuously improving

Building Momentum

The first phase is about building the business case, obtaining commitment, and building the velocity required to make a significant change. To begin, the team should identify what the current culture and values are, working closely with key decision makers within a company and evaluating the business's current organizational health and maturity. This can be obtained through interviews with key employees and executives or by utilizing surveys for data collection. This should provide enough information to use as a guideline to measure the improvement against and also provide you with the key drivers that are present in your current culture. Once you've obtained the key drivers, you can begin to build your plan for improvement, ensuring there is a narrative that all employees can relate to, not just upper or middle management. This includes how you plan to manage and monitor the program, cost, communication, and risk. Once the plan is completed, you will have a clear picture of what the future organizational culture is to look like, and this is what you will use to gain buy-in, as this process requires leadership endorsement and buy-in. You can then proceed with saturating the work environment with culture messages, focusing primarily on the culture story, reinforcing values, and empowering employees to act on those values. Seeing and sharing these messages leads to new conversations, both internally and within the larger community.

At the conclusion of phase 1, you should have the following in place:

- A clear outline of the current corporate culture and ideal culture
- A sponsored and endorsed plan for change
- A communication strategy and plan for the cultural change
- Commitment by the board, CEO, and key executives to take on the journey

Changing Mindsets

The second phase of cultural change is the actual change itself. This is the most difficult phase, as employees often fear or are resistant to change. During this period, you will focus on placing key enablers to lead the culture into the future. Training and changing the beliefs and values of current leaders will be extremely important during this phase, as will be hiring new employees that are more in line with the culture you wish to create. There will also come a point during this phase where it might be necessary to let go of those who are not in line or in agreement with the culture change or who cannot adapt. It is also at this step where true change must occur. If you do not see the required change in the majority of your senior leadership, where they consistently display the needed traits and are role models for the rest of the organization, you must continue to do what is necessary to shift the culture, and only once you are confident that you have in fact achieved the change should you move forward to the third step. Expect the transition to take some time, as some workers will get used to the change faster than others. It is also during the second phase when you will reach a point when those leaders in charge of major processes should use the feedback from their learning to improve or redesign those processes to ensure that they are reflective of the desired culture.

At the conclusion of phase 2, you should have the following in place:

- New cultural behaviors being displayed in most employees, with leaders serving as role models for the rest of the organization
- Any needed performance management changes designed
- New rituals, meetings, and activities that support the values and behaviors
- A flurry of communications using various methods to reinforce desired behaviors and update the community on status

Continuously Improving

In the third phase, the goal is continuous improvement, in the sense that the change is reinforced but you are also refining the processes to improve and accelerate your transformation. By continuing to use the new behaviors, procedures, and models that were created during the change to a model of process-based thinking, it is less likely that your company will revert to old habits. It is also within the third phase that you will once again measure the success of the program, continue communicating desired behavior and values, and evaluate who within the company will disrupt the progress of the program and who are capable of making the change. At the end of this phase, everyone should be able to clearly articulate the positive culture change within the company, and how their actions impact and reinforce it. By valuing Kaizen—a Japanese philosophy of continuous improvement often used in business—cultural change can bring significant advancement to a company.

At the conclusion of phase 3, you should have the following in place:

- Everyone trained in the new value system and fully bought in to the new corporate vision
- Everyone articulating the unique aspects about the culture
- Everyone understanding how what they and others do builds and reinforces that culture
- Evidence of a competitive advantage in both the customer and employment market based on the corporate culture
- Everyone looking to continually find ways to improve work, life, and operations

The path from one phase to the next is rarely straightforward. Most companies relapse at some point and recycle through certain phases. In fact, relapse is common, perhaps even inevitable, and so we urge you not to be discouraged by it, but to think of it as an integral part of the cultural change process. You will learn something about the company or department each time it relapses, and the next time, you can use what you learned, adapt, and be even stronger as you continue on the pathway to change.

WHAT ARE THE COMPONENTS OF A GREAT CULTURE?

Cultural principles are tested, modified, adapted, and transmitted by the entire company. But it all needs to start somewhere. Since every company is different, there are many ways to develop a culture that works. There are several principles that companies should consider in order to create a healthy corporate culture, and isolating those elements can be the first step toward building a differentiated culture and a lasting organization (Figure 6.4).

CULTURE

PRINCIPLES OF A HEALTHY CORPORATE CULTURE

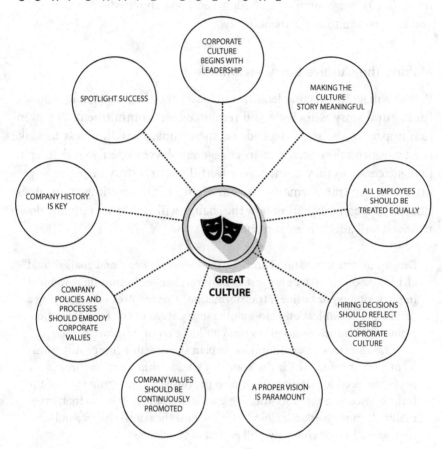

FIGURE 6.4
Principles of a healthy corporate culture.

Corporate Culture Begins with Leadership

Leaders need to explain and share their vision of the company's future with their workers. A company without a vision is reactive in nature, and its management is seldom confident in addressing competitive threats and stepping into the future. In addition, leaders should be aware that their own behaviors and attitudes set the standard for the entire workforce. Managers who set poor examples in areas such as business or personal ethics, lifestyle, dedication to quality, and dealings with colleagues, customers, vendors, or employees will almost certainly find their companies defined by such characteristics. Building a strong and committed executive team is hard. To harness the transformative power of the senior leadership team, CEOs must often make tough decisions about who has the ability and enthusiasm to make the journey.

Making the Culture Story Meaningful

People will go to amazing lengths for causes they believe in, and a powerful cultural story will create and reinforce their commitment. The eventual impact of the story depends on the company's willingness to make the transformation personal, to engage employees openly, and to spotlight successes as they emerge. A powerful cultural story helps employees believe in the transformation by answering their most important questions, which can range from how the change will affect the company down to how it will affect them personally.

Before any transformation launches, the vision, strategy, and goals should all be in place. This is true not just for cultural changes, but any improvement implementation or business transformation. This involves incorporating a detailed communication plan guiding every stage of the transformation, from initial launch to sustaining and building on the improvement.

A transformation's communication plan starts with a compelling transformation story in which the company's leadership team summarizes a profound need for change, while also providing an inspiring view of the future, cascading the story through each management layer so that, eventually, all employees understand why and how they must change, and what they, as well as the company, will get out of the change.

All Employees Should Be Treated Equally

Organizations should ensure all employees are treated equally. This does not mean that you can't present extra rewards to workers who excel, but it does mean that all interactions with employees should be based on a foundation of mutual respect.

Hiring Decisions Should Reflect Desired Corporate Culture

A mature company ensures it hires workers who will treat clients and fellow employees well and dedicate themselves to mastering the tasks for which they are responsible. A good attitude is an essential component of any healthy corporate culture. But managers also need to make sure that hiring decisions are not based on ethnic, racial, or gender issues. Businesses benefit from having a diverse workforce rather than one that is overly homogeneous.

Two-Way Communication Is Essential

Managers who discuss problems openly with their employees and enlist their help in solving them will likely be rewarded with a healthy working environment. This can be a critical asset, for once a participatory and engaging culture has been established, it can assist with propelling a company ahead of its competition. Conversely, problems with corporate culture can play a major role in organizational failures. When employees only perform the tasks necessary to do their own jobs, rather than putting out extra effort on behalf of the overall business, productivity declines and growth slows. Many companies tend to ignore the developing cultures within their businesses until it is too late to make any needed changes.

A Proper Vision Is Paramount

A great culture starts with a vision. A vision statement is often quite simple, but it ultimately guides a company's values and provides it with purpose. That purpose, in turn, orients every decision employees make. When they are deeply authentic and prominently displayed, good vision statements can even help align customers, suppliers, and other stakeholders with the company's cultural norms and expectations. A vision statement is a simple but foundational element of culture.

Company Values Should Be Continuously Promoted

A company's values are the core of its culture. While a vision articulates a company's purpose, values offer a set of guidelines on the behaviors and mindsets needed to achieve that vision. Clearly articulated sets of values are prominently communicated to all employees and involve the way that firm vows to serve its clients, treat colleagues, and uphold professional standards. The originality of values is less important than their authenticity.

Company Policies and Processes Should Embody Corporate Values

Of course, values are of little importance unless they are enshrined in a company's policies and processes. Whatever an organization values, it must be reinforced in review criteria and promotion policies and baked into the operating principles of daily life in the firm.

Company History Is Key

Any organization has a unique history and a unique story. The ability to unearth that history and craft it into your cultural narrative, mission, and values is a core element of culture creation and change. The elements of your cultural narrative can be formal or informal, but in any case, they are powerful tools when identified, shaped, and retold as a part of a firm's ongoing culture mission.

There are numerous other factors that influence culture, but the components outlined above can provide a firm foundation for shaping a new organizational philosophy.

Spotlight Success

As the company's cultural transition progresses, a powerful way to reinforce the transformation is to spotlight its successes. Sharing success stories helps crystallize the meaning of the transformation and brings people confidence that it will actually work. Show other people successes and that such behavior is valued and goes a long way.

Some warning signs of trouble with company culture include increased turnover, difficulty in hiring talented people, low attendance at company events, a lack of honest communication and understanding of the company mission, and us versus them mentality between employees and management or within different departments, and declining quality and customer satisfaction. A company exhibiting one or more of these warning signs should consider whether the problems stem from the company culture. If so, your organization should take steps to improve its culture, including reaffirming the company's mission and goals and establishing a more open relationship with employees.

HOW TO CHANGE THE BEHAVIORS OF OTHERS

Our daily lives are often a series of habits played out through the day, a limited reality fettered by the slow accumulation of our previous actions. But habits can be changed, as difficult as that may seem sometimes. Although changing the behavior of others can be one of the most difficult tasks of cultural change, it can also be one of the most rewarding. There are several ways to facilitate the change, and once momentum has been achieved, people will become more engaged with the new culture and new cultural norms will begin to appear. There are many techniques used to assist in changing the behavior of others. We will review three:

1. Ways to influence people's beliefs and values
2. Ways to influence people's feelings
3. Ways to influence people's level of awareness

Ways to Influence People's Beliefs and Values

There are multiple ways to influence the values and beliefs of your people so that they are aligned with the culture you wish to build. These include

- Exposure to others who have been successful. This can include mentoring programs, reading books that relate to successful culture changes, or even sending employees to conferences and training.
- Hiring new people. This can include selecting individuals from an organization that has the desired culture you want or hiring individuals that you have worked with in the past that you trust, are flexible, and exhibit the behaviors and values you seek.

Ways to Influence People's Feelings

How someone feels has a high impact on how he or she operates in his or her daily life and routine. We are influenced by our motivation toward something, whether positive or negative.

- Increasing positive motivation could include being valued and receiving recognition for something that you've completed, helping others, for example, to support and develop those within your team, and making a difference in your organization. By increasing positive motivation, you can thus increase one's engagement and satisfaction. This changes our outlook on how we feel within a company and the value we provide.
- Decreasing negative motivation is extremely important in the new culture that you develop. This could include eliminating or decreasing mistrust, lack of accountability, fear of change, fear of making a mistake, and bullying. All of these items can cause an individual to become defensive, and as a result, they will become resistors to change. It is important to set clear goals and purposes, and to ensure employees are rewarded and provided with the proper support, structure, and guidance.

Ways to Influence People's Level of Awareness

To influence one's level of awareness, we need to be mindful of keeping the balance in the organization. This can include

- Maintaining proper work–life balance
- Ensuring people take their vacation time
- Having flexible working hours
- Holding regular team workshops, town halls, and conferences
- Creating opportunities to move within the organization
- Coaching and mentoring opportunities
- Conducting regular performance reviews

Employees who are willing to change their behavior may also see that the principles of process improvement will help them continue to make more changes that will bring them an increasing level of value. Being self-aware is a very important state as you understand your strengths and weaknesses and are aware of your emotions. These individuals can be excellent resources when you are attempting to change the culture of your organization. Employees who have a high level of self-awareness also have an increased sense of well-being and thus

- Have a realistic view of situations
- Are accepting of others and themselves

- Have an ability to see things in a different light
- Have a high self-esteem and are not quick to judge
- Are open to new ideas

Through making changes willingly, these employees may move up in the company, be able to do more work with less effort, or engage in new tasks and learn something they have always been interested in knowing. This adds value to their life, to the company they work for, and to the customers of that company. With process-oriented thinking and a customer-centric focus, behavioral changes can be significant.

HOW DOES LEADERSHIP PLAY A ROLE IN PROCESS IMPROVEMENT?

When a company makes a change toward process orientation, that company's leadership also has to change. Good leadership is always needed in process improvement, but so often it is the lacking element. Leaders should connect the process and the people, and if they do it right, it can be amazing for the entire organization. If they do not know how to do it, or are not committed to doing it, process orientation and focus will generally just fall apart, and the culture will start to revert back to the one that was seen before change was undertaken.

One of the surest ways to align culture to the organization's strategy is to ensure leadership practices are universally aligned and accepted. Leaders, at all levels, need to understand what the desired culture is and then determine ways of establishing practices and procedures in all areas of the business that will closely reflect that culture. They also need to act as role models and consistently display the very behaviors they wish to be exhibited by everyone in the organization, while also providing the necessary support to others that will enable them to function accordingly. Figure 6.5 illustrates various leadership behaviors and the culture they produce.

Leadership is the action of leading a group of people or an organization.

While many tools exist to help employees work in a more process-oriented environment, the full benefits are not seen without the proper

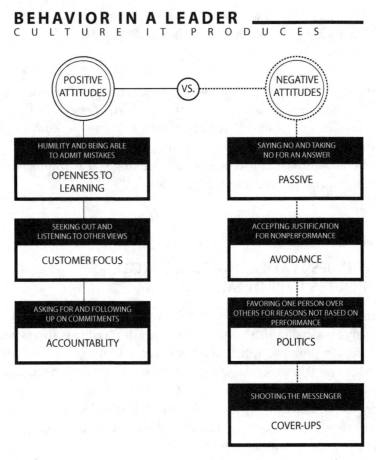

FIGURE 6.5
Leadership behaviors and the culture they produce.

leadership to go with those tools. The reduction of wasted effort and finding better ways for employees to get their work done are important parts of process-oriented thinking, but there is more to a process-oriented company than just that. Process-focused leadership is about enabling and empowering people. It is about helping people grow professionally and personally, allowing them to take pride in their work. Process-focused leaders don't hide in their offices; they spend time coaching people, leading people, and seeing what is actually happening with their people as they conduct their work, rather than simply managing metrics and reading reports.

A leader in a process-focused company

- Ensures that each employee takes initiative to solve problems and improve his or her job or operating environment
- Ensures that each person's job is aligned to provide value for the customer and prosperity for the company
- Manages processes and performance, not reports and numbers
- Teaches colleagues and employees that financial results are the result of processes
- Doesn't jump to conclusions or solutions, but tries to understand the situation, ask why, and perform root cause analysis
- Focuses on the work and problem at hand, avoiding finger-pointing and placing blame
- Ensures actions of all employees revolve around planning and problem solving
- Understands that hiding problems will undermine the organization and its performance and potential
- Understands what customers want, need, and value, or what will thrill them
- Understands that open, trustworthy, and frequent communication builds trust and encourages open problem solving

Sustaining a cultural shift to a process improvement culture requires a change in mindset and behavior across leadership, and then gradually throughout the organization. Process improvement successes truly occur when senior leaders put appropriate structures and processes in place and get personally involved in sustaining the cultural conversion, such as learning about process improvement and developing other process-driven leaders throughout the enterprise. Process improvement is surprisingly different from conventional leadership, as it emphasizes visibly observable discipline and accountability. Unlike other approaches to management, process improvement provides the templates and practices that enable leaders to learn, and then look for, ask about, and reinforce the leadership behaviors that sustain the gains. When leadership establishes the elements of process improvement, engages consistently in the process improvement initiatives, and adopts it as an important element in their organization's strategy and approach, benefits will accrue. Figure 6.6 describes 10 things process-oriented leaders do to differentiate themselves from traditional managers.

LEADERSHIP

10 THINGS PROCESS ORIENTED LEADERS DO

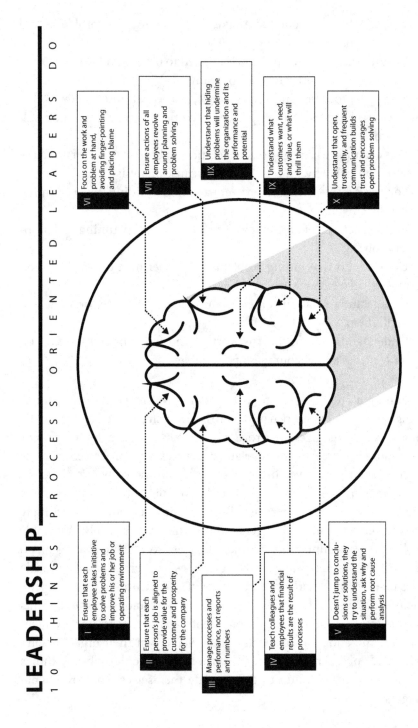

I Ensure that each employee takes initiative to solve problems and improve his or her job or operating environment

II Ensure that each person's job is aligned to provide value for the customer and prosperity for the company

III Manage processes and performance, not reports and numbers

IV Teach colleagues and employees that financial results are the result of processes

V Doesn't jump to conclusions or solutions, they try to understand the situation, ask why and perform root cause analysis

VI Focus on the work and problem at hand, avoiding finger-pointing and placing blame

VII Ensure actions of all employees revolve around planning and problem solving

VIII Understand that hiding problems will undermine the organization and its performance and potential

IX Understand what customers want, need, and value, or what will thrill them

X Understand that open, trustworthy, and frequent communication builds trust and encourages open problem solving

FIGURE 6.6
Ten things process-oriented leaders do.

WHAT ROLE DOES HR PLAY IN
PROCESS IMPROVEMENT?

Getting employee matters right is essential for any serious process-driven transformation, particularly because the primary goal of process improvement is to help people achieve more, build their capabilities, increase their capacity, and intensify their engagement with colleagues and customers. Organizations that successfully engage their HR department throughout their application of process improvement see significant long-term advantages. In many cases, where HR is not a mutually supportive partner, the transition to process-driven thinking tends to struggle. From the front line up to senior leaders, process improvement creates new roles and changes old ones significantly as the organization breaks down internal silos and redesigns its operating patterns and procedures. Securing HR support from the beginning of your process journey is key. Here are six ways your HR department can assist with your process-driven transformation:

1. *Implementing new organizational structures*: The redeployment of both managers and employees will require collaboration from HR in order for the transformation to take hold. HR's support in identifying and staffing a stable management team and ensuring they are committed to the new emphasis on coaching and feedback, rather than just technical competence, will be crucial to reinforce the changes. If one of the goals of the transformation is to free up substantial human capacity, HR can assist with finding morale-boosting redeployment opportunities for those effected by the changes. Before the transformation starts, basic HR steps, such as winding down contracts for contingent workers, reducing recruiting efforts, and improving transparency and communication about open positions, can underscore the organization's commitment to its employees.

2. *Communicating and monitoring employee responses*: Changes in leadership, team structure, and performance standards can be deeply stressful for frontline employees and middle managers. That leads to HR's next major contribution, which is to help with communicating the transformation, monitoring employee reactions to it, and addressing concerns that arise.

3. *Integrating process improvement into the talent system*: Among the most visible legacies of a process-oriented transformation are the tools and

practices that are used and displayed across the organization. These include skills matrices, coaching instructions, and performance–dialogue formats—which fundamentally redesign how people do their work and engage with customers and colleagues. When executed consistently, the result is a new set of cultural norms.

4. *Recruiting*: The most forward-thinking organizations recognize that instilling process improvement values in employees begins before they are hired, when defining the role profiles of ideal job candidates. HR will therefore need to update corporate collateral job descriptions and other related documents to incorporate process improvement characteristics and behaviors. Likewise, recruiting teams and interviewers may require training so that they understand and recognize important process improvement skills, such as asking candidates more about their experience on high-performance teams or how they encountered and solved performance problems in the past.

5. *People development*: People development will undergo a significant change as individual and team performance becomes transparent throughout the organization. Structures designed around burdensome or high-stress, annual or semiannual review processes must evolve to support frequent, everyday conversations about how work is progressing and where it could be improved. Throughout the organization, people from the CEO down to the front line will need to be assessed on how well they follow and role-model process improvement practices. Managers and executives should be evaluated on their commitment to changing their performance styles and schedules to emphasize feedback and coaching, while frontline workers should continuously demonstrate root cause problem solving and a process improvement mindset.

6. *Prevention of ambiguity wastes*: Karen Martin and Mike Osterling outlined an accompanying category to the traditional wastes of an organization that focuses on eight additional areas where significant confusion and wasted effort could occur if proper expectations are not clear to all members of a company. These include terminology and communication, problem solving and decision making, work systems, roles and responsibilities, policies, business goals and priorities, customers and products, and organizational purpose and vision (Figure 6.7). Ambiguity, lack of clarity, or a failure to plan in any of these key areas is a plan for failure in the modern organization. As simple as it sounds, failure to understand where you are, what you

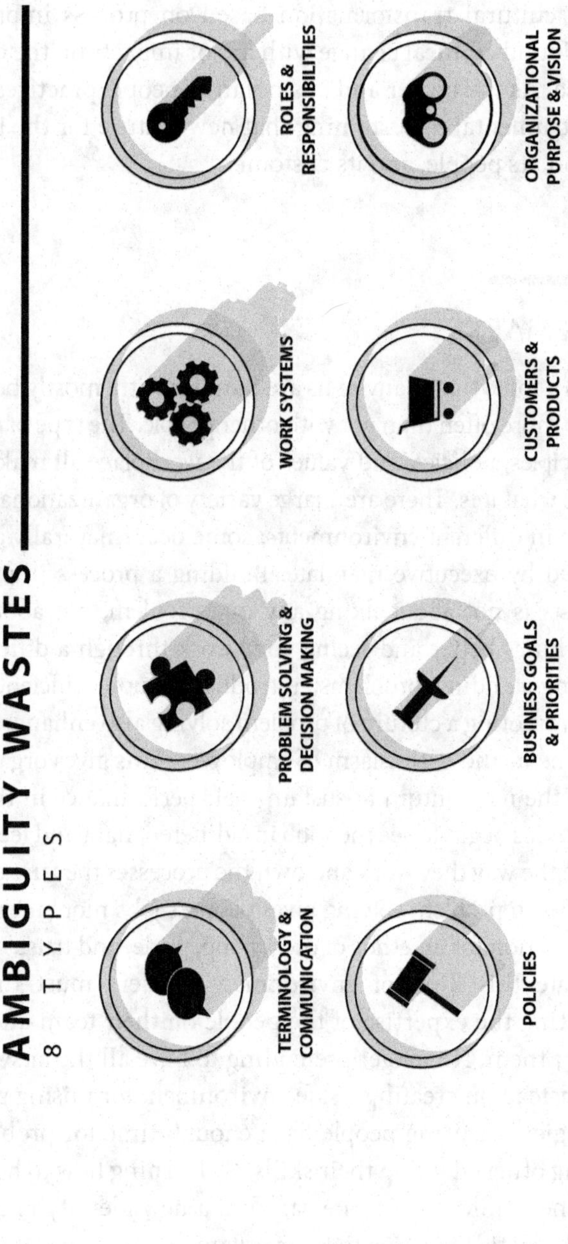

AMBIGUITY WASTES
8 TYPES

TERMINOLOGY & COMMUNICATION

PROBLEM SOLVING & DECISION MAKING

WORK SYSTEMS

ROLES & RESPONSIBILITIES

POLICIES

BUSINESS GOALS & PRIORITIES

CUSTOMERS & PRODUCTS

ORGANIZATIONAL PURPOSE & VISION

FIGURE 6.7
Eight types of ambiguity waste.

196 • *The Basics of Process Improvement*

want, who your customers are, how to communicate effectively, who is responsible for what, and what restrictions or constraints exist in any given work environment will almost guarantee wasted resources and ultimately hinder or prevent the outcomes you hope to achieve.

A successful cultural transformation based on process improvement produces a profound cultural change with major impacts on the organization's workforce. As the owner and custodian of people practices, the HR function is instrumental to sustaining that new culture for the benefit of the organization, its people, and its customers.

CLOSING REMARKS

Work culture is a topic that many of us are familiar with, mostly because we work, and do so more often than not with other people. The type of organization, staff, principles, policies, and values of the workplace all make organizational culture what it is. There are a large variety of organizational cultures that materialize in different environments; some occur naturally and some are implemented by executive mandate. Building a process improvement culture that lasts is not about fixing any one problem, but about always striving to do things better and seeing your work through a different lens. Eliminating long-standing problems, introducing more efficient ways of working, and promoting a culture of problem solving also enhance the capabilities, engagement, and enthusiasm of employees. This gives organizations the means and the momentum to sustain their performance in the future. Frontline employees begin to see their job in a different light and feel empowered to improve the way they work and own the processes they use every day. Taking part in team problem solving gives people's jobs more meaning and creates the foundation for an ethos of ownership, pride, and trust.

To help create this kind of environment, leaders must themselves change, respecting the expertise of the people on their team and finding ways to support them. No longer pretending to have all the answers, they should focus instead on creating a safe environment for raising problems, defining strategies, ensuring people have enough time for problem solving, and helping others develop their skills. By learning how to help others contribute to their fullest, everyone can find a new identity and an even more powerful way to add value to their organization.

7

Conclusion

For many organizations, the goal of sustained improvement has been at least as frustrating as attractive. But in an era when time-to-value pressures have been elevated, the simplicity of improvement initiatives and the use of basic improvement tools and techniques are paramount. In all industries, each generation of business leaders hopes to discover a combination of business strategies and operating techniques that foster economic growth for their business, and personal reward for themselves as well as the company's employees. Leaders who have recognized how much can be achieved when they unleash the power of process improvement are the ones whose organizations are performing to their fullest potential. The most successful organizations, whether in technology, finance, telecommunications, or the public sector, are those that deeply commit to the disciplines of process improvement. They unlock employees' problem-solving capabilities. They ensure that everyone from the front line to the CEO knows how to see problems, solve them, and push the organization to improve. They possess the flexibility to respond to changing market demands and deliver what customers value as efficiently as possible. Lastly, they are the ones with the greatest sense of purpose, where their employees understand where the company is going and possess the skills, knowledge, and tools to help get it there.

Over the years, we have watched, and used, many process-oriented tools and techniques, and we still believe most are aimed at the same benefits: faster time to market, reduced wastage, lower inventories, and higher productivity. Today more than ever, organizations worldwide, from manufacturers to hospitals, to banks, to technology companies, to governments, are making a difference by adopting process-driven philosophies, mindsets, and methodologies. Delivering value efficiently to the customer, enabling people to lead and contribute to their fullest potential, discovering better ways of working, and connecting strategy and goals through process orientation can help transform entire organizations, from the front line to the executive suite.

The purpose of *The Basics of Process Improvement* was to explain the primary underpinnings of process improvement and how it can assist any organization to mature, evolve, and improve. Our mission was to present process improvement techniques from a simple and straightforward perspective that integrated diverse and sometimes forgotten concepts in a novel manner. The hope was that by outlining the essentials of process improvement, we could remind people of its importance and reinspire individuals to embark on a process-driven journey.

EACH CASE IS DIFFERENT

The discussions in this book centered on building a mindset of process improvement and providing a wide-sweeping toolkit that you could reference and use as needed in your day-to-day job. By keeping principles such as common sense and simplicity in mind, you can use the techniques and lessons in this book to help you solve difficult problems, design better solutions, and transform processes in a much easier fashion. When it comes to organizational transformation, we don't think the challenge is to learn modern methods or use sophisticated technologies to solve everyday problems, but rather to ignore them in many cases so that you can focus on the very few, but proven practices in the industry. Yes, leading-edge trends are significant and are certainly useful to understand, but true improvement is not about technology or methodology alone. The art of process improvement transcends technology and methodology and enables individuals to remove walls and see work in a different light, to solve a problem, improve operations, or transform themselves or their company in a meaningful and long-lasting way.

CRITICAL SUCCESS FACTORS

Since each organization has differing cultures and priorities, it is important to remember that process improvement is one element of the continual

CONCLUSION
CRITICAL SUCCESS FACTORS

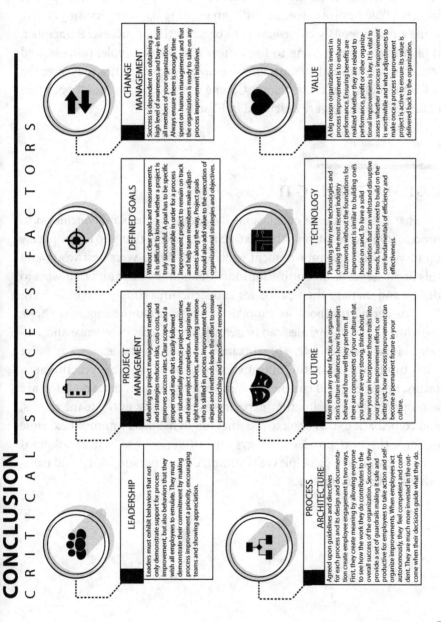

LEADERSHIP

Leaders must exhibit behaviors that not only demonstrate support for process improvement, but also behaviors that they wish all employees to emulate. They must demonstrate their commitment by making process improvement a priority, encouraging teams and showing appreciation.

PROJECT MANAGEMENT

Adhering to project management methods and strategies reduces risks, cuts costs, and improves success rates. Clear scope, and a proper road map that is easily followed can substantially enhance project outcomes and ease project completion. Assigning the right team members, and ensuring someone who is skilled in process improvement techniques and methods leads the effort to ensure proper coaching and impediment removal.

DEFINED GOALS

Without clear goals and measurements, it is difficult to know whether a project is truly successful. A goal has to be specific and measurable in order for a process improvement project to remain on track and help team members make adjustments along the way. Project goals should also add value to the execution of organizational strategies and objectives.

CHANGE MANAGEMENT

Success is dependent on obtaining a high level of awareness and buy-in from all members of your organization. Always ensure there is enough time spent on human management and that the organization is ready to take on any process improvement initiatives.

PROCESS ARCHITECTURE

Agreed upon guidelines and directives for each process and its design and documentation create employee engagement in two ways. First, they create meaning by allowing everyone to see how the work they do contributes to the overall success of the organization. Second, they provide a set of guardrails making it safe and productive for employees to take action and self-organize improvements. When employees act autonomously, they feel competent and confident. They are much more invested in the outcome when their decisions guide what they do.

CULTURE

More than any other factor, an organization's culture influences how its members behave and how well they perform. If there are components of your culture that you know are very strong, think about how you can incorporate those traits into your process improvement efforts, or better yet, how process improvement can become a permanent fixture in your culture.

TECHNOLOGY

Pursuing shiny new technologies and chasing the most recent industry buzzwords without the foundations for improvement is similar to building one's house on sand. To have a solid foundation that can withstand disruptive trends, businesses need to build on the core fundamentals of efficiency and effectiveness.

VALUE

A big reason organizations invest in process improvement is to enhance performance. Ensuring benefits are realized whether they are related to performance, profit or other organizational improvements is key. It is vital to assess whether a process improvement is worthwhile and what adjustments to make once a process improvement project is active to ensure its value is delivered back to the organization.

FIGURE 7.1
Critical success factors.

change process inherent in organizational transformation. Solid planning, ample involvement of those affected by change, and an openness to build collaborative solutions are critical success factors for achieving optimal success. True improvement provides an exciting opportunity for growth, while simultaneously contributing to organizational success. Remember, if organizations are going to implement successful people, process, and technology change, they must enable employees and ensure they have the skills to implement those changes. Some of the other key success factors outlined in the book are described in Figure 7.1.

JUST START DOING IT

So what is the ultimate conclusion? By design, there is no conclusion to process improvement, only the next step, and taking that step is completely up to you. Process improvement is all about doing your best work, and this book serves as an outline for individuals and companies that wish to design and manage their processes and structures simply and effectively. By considering this book as a toolkit of new and old principles, we hope individuals and companies can better achieve process excellence and sustained improvement. Every organization has unique challenges, and we've tried to present all of the information we think can help practitioners, teams, managers, and customers. Apply the techniques that you think are appropriate for your situation, experiment constantly, evaluate the results, and come back to this book to see what might help you improve next time or solve the next problem. Always aim to design and deliver solutions while allowing the principles of restraint, discipline, simplicity, and naturalness to be your guide.

To Learn More

Sources for *The Basics of Process Improvement* include:

Books

Boutros, Tristan, and Tim Purdie. *The Process Improvement Handbook: A Blueprint for Managing Change and Increasing Organizational Performance.* New York: McGraw-Hill Education, 2013.

Garimella, Kiran K. *The Power of Process: Unleashing the Source of Competitive Advantage.* Tampa, FL: Meghan-Kiffer, 2006.

Harrington, James. *Business Process Improvement: The Breakthrough Strategy for Total Quality, Productivity, and Competitiveness.* New York: McGraw-Hill, 1991.

Imai, Masaaki. *Gemba Kaizen: A Commonsense Approach to a Continuous Improvement Strategy.* 2nd ed. New York: McGraw-Hill, 2012.

Jacka, J. Mike, and Paulette J. Keller. *Business Process Mapping: Improving Customer Satisfaction.* Hoboken, NJ: John Wiley & Sons, 2009.

Jeston, John, and Johan Nelis. *Business Process Management: Practical Guidelines to Successful Implementations.* Burlington, MA: Butterworth-Heinemann, 2006.

Martichenko, Robert. *Everything I Know about Lean I Learned in First Grade.* Cambridge, MA: Lean Enterprise Institute, 2008.

Martin, Karen, and Mike Osterling. *Value Stream Mapping: How to Visualize Work and Align Leadership for Organizational Transformation.* New York: McGraw-Hill Education, 2013.

McDonald, Mark. *Improving Business Processes: Expert Solutions to Everyday Challenges.* Boston: Harvard Business, 2010.

Morgan, John, and Martin Brenig-Jones. *Lean Six Sigma for Dummies.* Chichester, UK: Wiley, 2012.

Panagacos, Theodore. *Ultimate Guide to Business Process Management: Everything You Need to Know and How to Apply It to Your Organization.* N.p.: CreateSpace Independent Publishing, 2012.

Schurter, Terry, and Peter Fingar. *The Insiders' Guide to BPM: 7 Steps to Process Mastery.* Tampa, FL: Meghan-Kiffer, 2009.

Sheridan, Richard. *Joy, Inc.: How We Built a Workplace People Love.* N.p.: Portfolio, 2015.

Taylor, Carolyn. *Walking the Talk: Building a Culture for Success.* London: Random House Business, 2005.

Viscardi, Stacia. *The Professional Scrum Master's Handbook: A Collection of Tips, Tricks, and War Stories to Help the Professional Scrum Master Break the Chains of Traditional Organization and Management.* Birmingham, UK: Packt, 2013.

Websites and Articles

American Society for Quality (AQS). Process view of work. Milwaukee, WI: ASQ. http://asq.org/learn-about-quality/process-view-of-work/overview/overview.html.

BMP Institute. The value of a formal business process repository. Westboro, MA: BMP Institute. http://www.bpminstitute.org/resources/articles/value-formal-business-process-repository.

Cook, Randy, and Alison Jenkins. Building a problem-solving culture that lasts. Cambridge, MA: Lean Management Enterprise. http://www.mckinsey.com/client_service/operations/latest_thinking/lean_management.

Frackleton, Erin, Girbig, Robert, Jacquemont, David, Singh, A.J. (2014) Guiding the people transformation: The role of HR in lean management. McKinsey & Company.

Grichnik, Kaj, Hans Bohnen, and Michael Turner. Standardized work: The first step toward real transformation. New York: Booz & Co. http://www.siue.edu/~mthomec/PTTools4_Process.pdf.

Marrelli, Anne F. The performance technologist's toolbox: Process mapping. *Performance Improvement* 44(5): 40–44. http://www.siue.edu/~mthomec/PTTools4_Process.pdf.

MindTools. Problem-solving skills. London: MindTools. http://www.mindtools.com/pages/main/newMN_TMC.htm.

Piper, David. Realizing process architecture. North Yorkshire, UK: Lamri Ltd., 2007. http://www.lamri.com/files/resources/Realizing%20Process%20Architecture.pdf.

University of Michigan. Process improvement methodology overview. Ann Arbor: University of Michigan. http://www.mais.umich.edu/methodology/process-improvement/.

Glossary

5S: Sort, straighten, shine, standardize, and sustain. Simple tool for organizing a workplace environment in a clean, efficient, and safe manner to enhance productivity and visual management and to ensure the introduction of standardized working.

5 Whys: Method for finding the root cause of issues by asking why at least five times.

8D problem solving: Eight disciplines (8Ds). Problem-solving method developed by the Ford Motor Company that is used to identify, correct, and eliminate recurring problems.

Activities: Activities in a process can be thought of as the actions that move the inputs through the process to become outputs.

Activity network diagram: Diagram of project activities that shows their sequential relationships using arrows and nodes.

Affinity diagram: Method for sorting information, ideas, or items into groups with similar characteristics. Invented by Kawakita Jiro, affinity diagrams are also known as K-J charts.

Arrows: Indicate the correct order or flow of a process and let readers follow flowcharts and other maps without a great deal of narrative explanation.

Attribute control chart: Type of control chart that evaluates the stability of a process by charting the count of occurrences of a given event in successive samples.

Benchmarking: Process for comparing internal results for a specific metric, such as cost, quality, or time, to the achievements of industry leaders for the purpose of improving the organization's own performance.

Brainstorming: A method for problem solving used by gathering ideas from a group in which the team generates as many ideas for potential solutions as possible in a defined period of time and in an orderly fashion presents them to the rest of the team.

Business processes: Processes that reflect the unique competencies of the enterprise and serve as the ultimate reason an organization exists.

Business process management system (BPMS): Central location for structuring and architecting processes and storing information about how an enterprise operates.

Check sheet: Form or method for collecting data in real time at the source. Check sheets, or recording tables, are matrices designed to assist in the tallying, recording, and analyzing test results or event occurrences.

Control chart: Used to indicate whether a process is in control and to help determine the cause of the variation.

Controls: Mechanisms placed on a process in order to ensure it is predictable, stable, and consistently operating at the target level of performance with only normal variation.

Coordinator: Full-time project participant who is elected to take notes at all meetings and provide those notes to participants.

Core and extended project teams: Teams responsible for delivery of daily project activities and actions. They regularly report on project status, issues, risks, open decisions, and dependencies.

Corporate behaviors: Behaviors of employees and their leadership that are most commonly displayed.

Corporate structures: Mechanisms by which a company manages tasks and people.

Corporate values: Values that employees associate meaning to and continually promote, and that drive what is occurring in a company.

Cross-functional map: Process map that provides richer information than a traditional flowchart. It can be expanded to show who does what, when tasks are done, and how long they take. Sometimes called a swim lane map.

CTQ tree: Critical-to-quality tree. Used to gather and organize a product's characteristics from the customer's point of view.

Culture: Corporate culture is commonly referred to as the shared attitudes, values, principles, and beliefs that characterize a company and define its nature and approach to managing employees, customers, investors, and the greater community.

Customers: Person, group, or department that benefits from the outputs of a process. Customers may be the actual consumer, but can also be in-house business units or outside business partners.

Cycle time: Time it takes for one item to make it from the beginning to the end of a process or step.

Data: Information that is used in or created by a created by a process.

Decision: Point in the process where a two-way branch occurs. For example, in a process for registering patients for hospital services, a decision point occurs regarding insurance. The question is, does the patient have insurance? If yes, the process branches to include steps for entering the insurance information, copying an insurance card, and verifying benefits. If no, the process branches instead to steps for entering self-pay information.

Defects: Product rejects and rework within your processes.

Design of experiments: Formal, planned experiments to uncover the effects of process change.

Dot plot: A simple chart showing data points on a relatively simple scale.

DRIVE: Acronym for an approach to problem solving and process improvement based on five steps (Define, Review, Identify, Verify, Execute).

Error proofing: Process of building safeguards into processes that reduce the possibility of mistakes or defects.

Executive committee: Highest level of oversight in a company's governance structure and is the driving force behind the organization's strategic plan.

Fishbone diagram: Visually represent the causes of a problem (or effect) and help determine the ultimate source of the problem—the root cause. Also called Ishikawa and cause-and-effect diagrams.

Flowchart: Visually represent relationships among the activities and tasks that make up a process.

Force field analysis: Framework for decisions that identifies forces driving toward an outcome or goal or forces that are blocking or driving away from the outcome.

Framework: A structure intended to serve as a support or guide for the building, improvement, or delivery of something that expands operations or delivers something useful or of value to an organization.

Governance: Establishment of policies, and continuous monitoring of their proper implementation, by the members of the governing body of an organization.

Histogram chart: Consist of vertical bars, side by side, that depict frequency distributions within tables of numbers and can help you understand data relationships over time (e.g., the familiar bell curve).

ICOR: Inputs, constraints, output, and resources. An internationally accepted process analysis methodology for process mapping.

Inputs: Things that are transformed by the process into an end product or service required by the customer of a process. These can be goods, ideas, or work items that enter the process in some raw form.

Interrelationship diagram: Shows how different issues are related to one another. It helps identify which issues are causing problems and which are an outcome of other actions. It also shows the strength of each influence.

Is/is not: Matrix that helps to precisely identify a problem by organizing known data and ideas about the problem into a table.

Linear regression: Regression analysis technique for modeling scalar relationships between a dependent variable and one or more independent variables.

Lower Control Limit (LCL): The bottom limit in quality control for data points below the control (average) line in a control chart. It is the opposite of upper control limit.

Management processes: Usually provide direction for an enterprise and exist to govern its operations. They are generally conducted by senior leaders to set organizational goals, develop visions, and deploy strategies, as well as establish and manage performance targets.

Narratives: Often included as callouts from mapping shapes on process maps, narratives give a short summary of actions and decisions.

Nominal group technique: More controlled form of brainstorming in which team members write down their ideas for subsequent discussion. Each team member writes ideas down independently, and then the group discusses the pros and cons of each idea.

Organized process team: Groups of people who work interdependently and cooperatively to meet customer needs or company goals.

Outputs: Can be products, services, or information and should conform to the specifications agreed to in advance with the customer of the process, whether they are internal or external.

Overprocessing: Overly elaborate and expensive equipment used to create products and services.

Overproduction: Manufacturing of products in advance or in excess of demand.

Pareto chart: Named after Vilfredo Pareto, who came up with the Pareto principle (or the 80/20 rule), the Pareto chart says that 20% of the factors account for 80% of potential problems.

Participants: People, groups, units, or departments that are involved in executing the process; usually defined as anyone who touches the process from the starting point to the finishing point.

Paynter chart: Chart that adds subgroupings to a Pareto chart to represent the run rate or frequency of specific variables.

Payoff matrix: Decision tool that uses numerical values assigned to possible outcomes to identify the optimum course of action. In it, each row represents a possible course of action and each column represents a possible state.

PDCA: Plan–do–check–act; sometimes seen as plan–do–check–adjust. Repetitive four-stage model for continuous improvement (CI) in business process management.

Policies: Set of basic principles and associated guidelines, formulated and enforced by the governing body of an organization, to direct and limit its actions in pursuit of long-term goals.

Prioritization matrix: Tool to prioritize diverse items into their order of importance by providing a score for each item.

Problem solving: Act of defining a problem; determining the cause of the problem; identifying, prioritizing, and selecting alternatives for a solution; and implementing a solution.

Problem-solving funnel: Method of identifying the root cause of a problem by moving from vague awareness that a problem exists through specific steps that narrow the focus and bring the organization to the root cause and possible solutions.

Procedure: Fixed, step-by-step sequence of activities or course of action (with definite start and end points) that must be followed in the same order to correctly perform a task.

Process: Sequence of linked tasks or activities that, at every stage, consume one or more resources (employee energy, time, infrastructure, machines, and money) to convert inputs (data, material, and parts) into outputs (products, services, or information).

Process architecture: Design and organization of business processes and related components into a unified structure and hierarchy.

Process components: Describe the various units of a process. Also known as process elements.

Process controls: Activities involved in ensuring a process is predictable, stable, and consistently operating at the target level of performance with only normal variation.

Process improvement: Refers to making a process more effective, efficient, or transparent.

Process improvement framework: Set of standards, methods, policies, and constraints used to help employees in different roles identify, measure, and improve the performance of the business processes that make up their company.

Process mapping: Step-by-step description of the actions taken by workers as they use a specific set of inputs to produce a defined set of outputs.

Process maturity: A concept used to assess an organization against a scale of five process maturity levels. Each level ranks the organization according to its standardization of processes in the area being assessed.

Process modeling: Like mapping, business process modeling allows teams to create pictures of processes within an organization, but it goes one step further by incorporating ideas such as economics, relationships, data, and business rules, and embeds these added layers into the visual diagram to create an all-encompassing profile.

Process-oriented architecture (POA): Occurs when all other architectures are centralized on the process of things rather than the specific business, service, data, or technology architecture. Although driven by process, POA is a model that strives to unify all architectures into one framework for optimal efficiency and understanding of an organization.

Process owner: Individual responsible for the day-to-day operation of the process—usually a supervisor, department head, or executive leader.

Project charter: Short document that lets the team know what the project is about and who will be involved.

Project selection matrix: Highlights elements for consideration when selecting and prioritizing projects, as well as for scoring, ranking, or prioritizing projects to determine which ones to undertake.

Process simulation: An instrument for the analysis of business processes. It is used to assess the dynamic behavior of processes over time, e.g., the development of process and resource performance in reaction to changes or fluctuations of certain environment or system parameters. The results provide insights to support decisions in process design or resource provision with the goal to improve factors such as process performance, process and product quality, customer satisfaction or resource utilization.

QMS review: Standardized review of an internal quality management system. International Organization for Standardization (ISO) certification and many industry standards require periodic reviews of quality systems and frameworks.

Radar chart: Graphical method for displaying small sets of multivariate data. Also known as a spider chart, each of the spokes represents one variable.

Relationship map: Shows dependencies between key processes by using labeled arrows to depict the inputs and outputs flowing between processes across an organization, along with its suppliers and customers.

Resources: All of the things that a process must routinely have to be able to convert inputs into outputs.

Responsibility chart (RACI): Matrix or diagram that shows responsibilities for activities in a project or process.

Risks: Perceived risks of a process, including waste, costs, and potential for errors or training issues. You would most likely record risks when mapping a desired state or future process with plans to make changes to existing workflows.

Run chart: Graph that displays observed data or variations in a time sequence. A simple, graphical representation of observed values in sequence.

Scatter diagram: Graph with different variables on the horizontal and vertical axes. Each data point is positioned on the graph at the intersection point of the two variables plotted on the respective axes. The result is a series of dots that show the distribution of data and the correlation of the variables.

SIPOC (sometimes COPIS): A tool that summarizes the inputs and outputs of one or more processes in table form. The acronym SIPOC stands for suppliers, inputs, process, outputs, and customers, which form the columns of the table.

Spaghetti diagram: Map of the production process from requirement to delivery. A complex map of the actual flow of an entire process, including all employee actions. The diagram gets its name from its frequent resemblance to a plate of spaghetti when it has been completed.

Sponsor: High-level individual with the ability to directly provide resources for a process or influence provision of resources, such as labor or capital.

Stakeholder map: Chart to analyze and identify key project influencers, which can help to win support for a project or improve the likelihood of its success by identifying stakeholder motivations.

Stakeholders: All other individuals contributing to the team effort or who have a vested interest in its outcomes.

Standard inventory: Inventory required to keep the process operating smoothly.

Standardization: Formulation and implementation of guidelines, rules, and specifications for common and repeated use, aimed at achieving optimum efficiency or uniformity in a process, organization, or system.

Statistical process control: Quality control method for monitoring a process to ensure it reaches its full potential for producing conforming products by eliminating or reducing waste, scrap, and rework.

Statistical sampling: Using a representative subset of a population to make inferences about the entire population.

Steering committee: A group of executives responsible for ensuring the optimal sequencing of activities and steering projects and programs in a positive manner as they relate to the broader enterprise strategy.

Subject matter expert (SME): Experienced or skilled employee of any level who provides information or guidance to the team.

Subprocess: Each step in a breakdown of a larger or complex process.

Supplier–customer relationship: Interface among internal organizations and external customers and suppliers of the organization.

Suppliers: Individuals, groups, vendors, or departments that provide inputs to a project—might include both in-house and outside entities.

Support processes: Exist to sustain the enterprise and support its core process backbone or value chain.

Survey: Tool used to gather information through polling or a questionnaire.

Swim lanes: Horizontal bands that show work activities in the context of each department responsible for executing a process.

SWOT analysis: Chart, typically shown with four quadrants, and, designed for rapid analysis of a market or competitive situation, accounting for organizational strength, weakness, opportunity, and threat.

Systems: Nonperson components of a process, including machines, automations, and computers.

Takt time: Rate at which products must be made, or services rendered in a process to meet customer demand.

Theory of constraints: Also known as TOC, this management method aims to maximize throughput by managing one or more constraining resources that impose limits on the entire process.

Tollgate review: Checkpoint to verify that all required activities have been completed before moving on to the next phase or project.

Transportation: Movement product or parts between manufacturing processes.

Upper Control Limit (UCL): A value that indicates the highest level of quality acceptable for a product or service. The upper control limit is used in conjunction with the lower control limit to create the range of variability for quality specifications, enabling those within the organization to provide an optimal level of excellence by adhering to the established guidelines.

Value stream map: Process improvement tool that outlines activities in high detail for every step of a process.

Vision: Optimal desired future state (the mental picture) of what an organization or process wants to achieve over time.

Waiting: Time when one process or activity waits to begin while another finishes.

Waste: Any resource consumed by inefficient or nonessential activities, any unwanted material left over from a production process, or any output that has no marketable value.

Workflow: Interrelated activities and resources deployed to execute a process.

Work in process (WIP): Work sequence and volume in which an operator performs tasks within takt time.

Index

Printed in the United States
by Baker & Taylor Publisher Services